21st
Century
Corbett

TITLES IN THE SERIES

21ST CENTURY FOUNDATIONS

Benjamin Armstrong, *editor*

In 1911 Capt. Alfred Thayer Mahan wrote in his book *Armaments and Arbitration,* "The study of military history lies at the foundation of all sound military conclusions and practices." One hundred years later, as we sail ever further into the twenty-first century, we are commonly told we face the most challenging circumstances in history, or that it is more dangerous now than ever before. These exaggerations tend to ignore the lessons of strategy and policy that come from our past.

The 21st Century Foundations series gives modern perspective to the great strategists and military philosophers of the past, placing their writings, principles, and theories within modern discussions and debates. Whether drawn from famous men or more obscure contributors with lesser known works, collecting and analyzing their writing will inform a new generation of students, military professionals, and policy makers alike. The essays and papers collected in this series are not provided in order to spell out cut and dry answers or exact procedures, but instead to help make sure we ask the right questions as we face the challenges of the future. The series informs the present by collecting and offering strategists and thinkers of the past.

21st Century Corbett

Maritime Strategy and Naval Policy for the Modern Era

Edited by Andrew Lambert

Naval Institute Press
Annapolis, Maryland

Naval Institute Press
291 Wood Road
Annapolis, MD 21402

Library of Congress Cataloging-in-Publication Data is available.

978-1-68247-168-5 (paperback)
978-1-68247-169-2 (eBook)

∞ Print editions meet the requirements of ANSI/NISO z39.48-1992 (Permanence of Paper).
Printed in the United States of America.

25 24 23 22 21 20 19 18 17   9 8 7 6 5 4 3 2 1
First printing

To the memory of a great historian

CONTENTS

Making National Strategy

Julian Stafford Corbett matters in the twenty-first century because he, like Carl von Clausewitz, understood that the key to making sound contemporary strategy lay in the combination of sophisticated historical analysis and strategic theory. While Clausewitz developed his texts for Prussia in the 1820s and Corbett for early twentieth-century Britain, both produced enduring insights for individuals facing similar tasks in other countries and other eras. Only a deep sustained and objective engagement with the past can provide the basis for current and future strategy; both men criticized the tendency to rely on a handful of catchphrases and heroic mythology. Both men were sophisticated historians at the cutting edge of contemporary professional methodologies. They achieved insight through sustained application to recovering the useful past. Only when they had assembled a substantial body of historical research did they begin to develop coherent national doctrine, and they did so by engaging with the best contemporary theoretical models.

Above all, both historians never lost sight of the unique, contingent nature of that task. Clausewitz never finished *On War*, and Corbett had no sooner published *Some Principles of Maritime Strategy* than he recognized the need to update it. These texts were living guides for war planning, strategy, and education and have to be read in that context. Understanding how these texts were created enables twenty-first-century strategists to follow in the footsteps of Corbett and Clausewitz; for experience must always take priority over theory because war is an art not a science.

Unlike Clausewitz, Corbett had to deal with the strategic problems of a unique maritime great power rather than a normative continental state dominated by armies, land borders, and regional concerns. He demonstrated that classical and contemporary strategy, dominated by land warfare, did not, as the British Army argued at the time, mean that Britain needed to copy Imperial Germany and create a mass conscript force. Britain, he demonstrated, was a sea power and depended on maritime (not solely naval) strategy to secure its global empire of trade, communications, investment, and influence. Corbett recognized that national strategy was set at the political level and rejected the idea that a single service could determine policy, as was the case in most pre-1914 Great Powers. The strategic doctrine he created enabled the British armed forces and civilian leadership to debate policy. When war broke out in August 1914 he would help direct the conflict and record the experience, roles that helped him to revise and refine national strategic doctrine. Above all, Corbett demonstrated that each nation needs a unique strategic doctrine that is based on history and theory, if it is to meet contemporary strategic needs. His insight remains as compelling now as it was a century ago.

In the last decades of the nineteenth century, rapid progress in military technology and portentous changes in the global political landscape forced nations to reconsider strategy and navies to grapple with the problem of preparing their officer corps for future wars. More than ever these processes required a solid theoretical base; there had been few contemporary conflicts to inform the development of tactical and operational doctrine, let alone strategic concepts. The U.S. Naval War College Newport was established in 1884 to address these issues—before the nation set to the task of building a new navy. In Great Britain the lack of strategic experience was compounded by the unique nature of the Imperial state—a diffuse collection of colonies, dominions, and informal economic zones and markets all bound together by seaborne and submarine telegraph communications. The entire system depended on sea control that was sustained by naval power. While many historians and thinkers addressed the tactical impact of new technology, and some adopted new strategic models, Corbett became the leading figure of the period because he went much further: He deployed law, history, and classical strategic theory—long dominated by continental military concerns—as well as a withering logic to analyze the unique situation of the British Imperial state. He produced strategic doctrine that used theory to stress the importance of the specific.

Corbett broke the mold of strategic writing by insisting on the primacy of national strategy, which must be soundly based in theory and integrate all aspects of national power under civilian direction: Navy, Army, communications, merchant shipping, economics, law, and culture.[1] As a civilian strategist whose experience of war was confined to a short season reporting on a conflict in the Sudan, where he saw nothing, and to a few naval maneuvers, which left him in raptures, his contribution would be intellectual. He never attempted to teach sailors or soldiers how to do their jobs; he only advised them on the higher purpose they served and, critically, on how to develop their own ideas. He taught the Royal Navy to think clearly and argue logically—critical tools for increasingly bitter defense debates driven by interservice rivalries and budgetary pressures. He believed the Navy was paramount, but needed an army to support national strategy. The attempt to create truly combined national strategy dominated his work and remains as relevant today as it was in Corbett's time. The Royal Navy lacked the intellectual equipment necessary to combat either the self-serving, aggressive claims of soldiers or the economizing intentions of legally trained politicians whose debating skills made them especially dangerous opponents for sea officers more familiar with oceans than advocacy.

Corbett's intellectual independence, his depth of historical understanding, and his legal background enabled him to analyze contemporary strategy with uncommon clarity and force. His work brought him into the contemporary defense debates. Building on the experience gained across a decade teaching strategy and history to midcareer and senior naval officers; providing intellectual coherence and rigor to internal naval memoranda on education, strategy, and policy; and generating lucid public statements of Admiralty policy, Corbett produced *Some Principles of Maritime Strategy*.[2] While the book has become the basis of all serious sea power theory, it was primarily a statement of contemporary British strategic doctrine; thus it focuses on fleets and major conflicts rather than constabulary duty and peace support missions.

Corbett's career can be read as a series of battles against those who would elevate a single armed service above the national interest, create doctrine out of dogma, abuse history to sustain their own ignorance, or weaken the nation's right arm—command of the sea. His elegant exposition, combining forensic legal skills with a fine literary style, moved strategic writing from the margins to the mainstream. Corbett educated the men who led the Royal Navy in the First World War: between 1914 and 1918 his Cabinet memoranda and Admiralty position papers helped shape the intellectual core of an evolving British war state, and he turned the experience of total war into an educational resource for the next generation.

His reputation has never stood higher. To this day historians of Tudor sea power, the Seven Years' War, the Napoleonic conflict, and the First World War consistently turn to him for strategic insight. Strategists and naval educators have kept *Some Principles* at the heart of curriculum, for that work remains the single most important text in the canon. Modern readings of Corbett are dominated by a sequence of books published between 1898 and 1922 that trace the evolution of British national strategy. Widely reprinted, these works remain highly accessible.

The Essayist

This volume supplements that rich strategic heritage with the best of Corbett's essays, works that had remained locked up in the dusty pages of long defunct journals. Unlike Captain Alfred Thayer Mahan, USN, who used the essay format as a major economic opportunity and wrote a great deal for that reason, Corbett had private wealth that allowed him the luxury of choice. He accepted challenging commissions and subjects of pressing national concern.

Corbett entered the contemporary naval controversies in 1907 because, as a civilian, he could see that the sustained attacks on First Sea Lord (1904 and 1910) Admiral Sir John Fisher's naval administration, were damaging the credibility of the Service. Fisher (1841–1920) was the most important British naval leader of the period. During his term as First Sea Lord, the professional head of the Navy and naval adviser to the government created the *Dreadnought*-type battleship and the battle cruiser, introduced oil fuel and the strategic use of wireless; invested heavily in submarines; improved officer education and the pay, conditions, and training of sailors; and improved gunnery. This program enabled Britain to win a major naval arms race with Imperial Germany. The negative, diffuse, and largely pointless arguments of the anti-Fisher group, "Syndicate of Discontent," were politically motivated and unsettling for a generation of politicians without any experience of war and for the wider public, who had taken British sea power for granted for a century. The "Syndicate" supported the Conservative Party, while Corbett and Fisher were Liberals. While Corbett did not agree with everything Fisher was doing, the "Syndicate" risked weakening the prestige of the Service that British deterrence rested on, reducing the Naval Estimates and even handing the direction of strategy to a self-serving continentalist Army. Corbett produced his first three major essays in 1907 to counter the claims of the Syndicate and the Army.

The essay format enabled him to engage in current controversies: he could push ideas and arguments to the limit, testing himself against the best minds of the day. Corbett, in contrast to many contemporary essayists, notably Mahan, recognized the relatively ephemeral nature of form. Consequently he did not collect his essays into book form. He preferred to develop his ideas in books. The first three essays in this collection, suitably shorn of polemical packaging, demonstrate Corbett's powerful contribution to current political and Service debate and his evolving grasp of the long-term demands of British strategy. These elements recur in all his mature works, not least in *Some Principles*, in which contemporary debates were pushed into the background. As an essayist Corbett preferred the counterattack; upon entering an active public debate he would master his brief, précis existing arguments, and develop a powerful case that exposed both the logical flaws and evidentiary failings of his opponents. All the essays in this collection had identifiable targets. This approach was consistent with his legal training and experience of advocacy. He was not a controversialist; he preferred the freedom of the longer format in which logic and evidence counted for more.

In these powerful, present-minded pieces Corbett pushed his arguments about strategy and policy into the heart of current political debates, targeting weak arguments, flawed logic, and inadequate evidence. He addressed senior officers and statesmen as well as professional historians and lawyers; he knew them all. He had worked with most of the senior officers of the Royal Navy, knew the leading academic historians of the day, and moved in the highest political circles. He was a member of a dining club known as the "Co-Efficients," an elite group of intellectuals with whom he debated the future of Britain and the empire. Fellow debaters included the secretary of state for war, the foreign secretary, radical *War of the Worlds* author H. G. Wells, geopolitical theorist Halford Mackinder, Imperial proconsul Alfred, 1st Viscount Milner, and playwright George Bernard Shaw. This forum helped crystallize Corbett's thinking about the national and imperial context of strategy. Further Corbett was closely connected to the political world—his elder brother was a member of Parliament, a City of London financier and, like Corbett himself, an early advocate of female suffrage. It is notable that Corbett's Liberal politics and progressive social views were distinctly at odds with those of his Service audience, with the exception of "Jacky" Fisher, the radical First Sea Lord 1904–1910.

Corbett's work would be profoundly influenced by his relationship with Fisher. Although very different characters, they understood that Britain had nothing to gain from a major military conflict and much to lose. They abhorred both war and excessive defense spending, preferring deterrence and arms racing to open conflict. They opposed Army attempts to establish a German-style mass conscript force, deeming it unnecessary, un-English, and uneconomic. Behind his alarming rhetoric, Fisher possessed a sophisticated mind—one that appreciated the brilliance of Corbett's work. In the first six months of 1907 Corbett produced three powerful essays that supported Fisher's policy, warship designs, and belligerent rights policy. These essays reflected Corbett's privileged access to the inner workings of the Admiralty and were based on his impressive contribution to advanced naval education on the Royal Naval War Course, the senior officer education program of the pre-1914 Royal Navy, in which he addressed theoretical and conceptual problems of creating and defining the strategy of a unique global maritime empire.

Fisher considered Corbett's 1907 publications—*England in the Seven Years' War* and the essays "Recent Attacks" and "The Capture of Private

Property at Sea"—to be defining literary outputs of the Edwardian age. The works established national strategy on maritime lines, that is as a combination of naval, military, and economic power, and demonstrated the wisdom of Fisher's program to secure peace with economy. Fisher had commissioned the essays and deployed Corbett's works as clinching arguments in his battles against Army khaki continentalism, Liberal internationalism, and conservative naval officers alarmed by the future.

His connection to Fisher placed Corbett at the heart of decision making in a great power anxious about "decline," the dissolution of empire—not least the future of Ireland—and increasing democratization. The Britain he wrote for faced the looming threat of a major European war sparked by the world power ambitions of Imperial Germany—ambitions made manifest by the expanding High Seas Fleet. Corbett recognized the need to ensure current debate was based on a sophisticated understanding of past practice, and he argued with legal rigor. As a public intellectual intimately engaged with naval and political circles at the highest levels, he knew the men in power, and they listened to his arguments.

Corbett's arguments bore the indelible stamp of his life. Born into a newly wealthy professional family in 1854, Corbett acquired a university education, a First Class degree in Law at Trinity College Cambridge, which reflected both the ambitions of his property-developer father and his own impressive intellectual capacity. He qualified as a barrister, a lawyer specializing in courtroom advocacy, but withdrew from legal practice in 1882 after his father's death to administer the family estate just outside London. His pastimes included local and national politics, travel, writing, and country sports. A hunting, shooting, and fishing man, Corbett was never happier than when in the saddle, following the hounds on a fast run over high hedges, taking salmon in Norway, or bringing home four hundred pheasant. Yet he spent every quiet moment reading and writing. In the 1880s and early 1890s Corbett produced some modestly successful novels, magazine articles, and plays. He moved in London intellectual circles, and included among his friends were Arthur Conan Doyle, Mark Twain, Henrick Ibsen, and the Macmillan publishing dynasty.[3] From the turn of the century, Corbett lived at Hans Crescent in the Knightsbridge district of London, often discussing politics and strategy with senior officers and statesmen while walking home through Green Park.

Corbett worked for the Royal Navy because he loved the Service and enjoyed the intellectual challenge. He did not need the money, cherishing the intellectual independence provided by family wealth. Like the British Empire he served, Corbett's family lived on the proceeds of major capital investments, combining a global portfolio and extensive London property holdings managed by his elder brother in the City of London, the epicenter of global capitalism. Corbett's background ensured he understood modern finance; not only was he personally enmeshed in the global financial system, but economic warfare occupied a prominent place on the Royal Navy War Course, where it informed the development of pre-war naval doctrine. Corbett's insights found expression in *Some Principles*, which clearly differentiated between contemporary economic warfare and the older concept of a physical blockade of the sailing era and emphasized that no government would miss an opportunity to undermine the "financial position on which the continued vigour of those armed forces so largely depends." Corbett also focused on the role of economic warfare in deterrence, a core concern of British strategic thinking: "If commerce and finance stand to lose by war, their influence for a peaceful solution will be great." He also stressed that the right to capture private property at sea was the key to British deterrence.[4] Corbett was equally well informed about the latest warfare and communications technology, submarines, aircraft, and dreadnoughts, along with the pressing need to integrate submarine telegraph cables and long-range wireless into British strategy.

Corbett's mastery of British strategy was acquired through a series of historical case studies developed from his Naval War Course lectures, which traced strategy evolution from the Tudors to Trafalgar and was informed by the latest experience from the Russo-Japanese War. These histories informed a sophisticated strategic synthesis, a "British" strategic doctrine that was equally as consistent with the classic texts of Clausewitz and Antoine Henri Jomini as it was with those of Mahan or Admiral Philip Colomb. This synthesis also demonstrated to contemporary British statesmen and senior officers the primacy of maritime power over continental strength in British practice. His maritime strategy was a sea-based synergy of naval and military power; he condemned naval strategy as a "minor" or operational issue. Corbett worked closely with successive directors of Naval Intelligence and directors of the Royal Naval War Course, those in the most influential positions in Admiralty war planning who attended his lectures and approved the publication of his national doctrine primer, *Some Principles*.[5]

The Royal Navy War Course

In 1902 the Royal Navy established a war course for mid-ranking and senior officers, emulating the American program at Newport. Corbett's role was to use history and strategic theory to teach his students that "expediency and strategy are not always in accord," an approach he categorized as "the deflection of strategy by politics."[6] This approach to Service education transformed his intellectual life. Corbett explained his aims in the introduction to a war course lecture in October 1903:

> Object of course to direct & assist private study.
> Practical Advantage of historical study the chief value a method of studying strategy.
> Difficulties of Strategical Study—no set rules ascertainable—continual conflict of expert opinion—not an exact science.
> Therefore difficult to do more than aim at acquiring strategical habit of thought.
> Here history is of greatest value.

In addition he offered a new definition of naval strategy, which was the minor form of national strategy and had "for its end the protection or destruction of commerce, or the furtherance or hindrance of military operations ashore." The Spanish Succession was chosen because it was "a useful study of a general European war to curb ambitious military power which had rapidly created a new navy."[7]

Corbett's approach remains critical in the twenty-first century. He told his students that naval strategy was the minor form of national strategy, concerned with "the protection or destruction of commerce, or the furtherance or hindrance of military operations ashore." The German challenge dominated the war course program, from lectures and war games to examination questions and course handouts. Corbett, like any capable Service educator, developed his teaching to address agendas set by the Service. His impact can be judged by the demand for additional lectures and the frequent requests for them at other naval bases. He was paid significantly more than other outside speakers and provided many more lectures: his fees accounted for half the Royal Navy's external speaker budget. Corbett knew what he was worth; he would happily have worked for nothing but not for a pittance.

The first fruit of this official connection was *England in the Mediterranean* of 1904, a text shaped by the secretary of the Committee of Imperial Defence (CID), the new civil/military body established to coordinate defense policy. The secretary, Colonel Sir George Sydenham Clarke was, despite his background in Army engineering, a leading exponent of maritime strategy. He helped Corbett shift from the detailed historical narrative of his earlier texts to an analytical, strategic approach. Thereafter Corbett's writing served the increasingly integrated needs of the war course, the Naval Intelligence Division, and the Committee of Imperial Defence. His lecture outlines were reproduced for students, while his books were intended not for the general public but, rather, for the naval and defense audience beyond the College.

After 1905 Corbett's analysis was heavily influenced by Clausewitz's *On War*, a text he used to sustain his argument that British strategy was maritime when he lectured at the Army Staff College at Camberley. The lectures for both Services reached a wider audience when *England in the Seven Years' War: A Study in Combined Strategy* was published in November 1907. For the first time Corbett appeared on the title page as "Lecturer in History to the Royal Naval War College." From the outset two things were abundantly clear. First, Corbett's book was a strategic analysis of a war that could only be understood by starting from "the naval side rather than from the military, as is more commonly done." Despite the numerous "brilliant actions" on the Continent and the relative lack of battles at sea, the study was "luminously informing" on the strategic use of the fleet and amphibious warfare, reducing Frederick the Great's activities to a subordinate role, as "an integral part of the maritime force with which it was primarily carried on." Second, his analysis was dominated by the application of Clausewitz's ideas to British maritime strategy. Well aware of the antitheoretical bent of the British mind, Corbett apologized for his theory-based strategic analysis. He argued, not entirely convincingly, that he employed such analysis because the true greatness of his characters could be seen only as they struggled with "the inexorable laws of strategy."

To ensure his work was seen in its proper context he thanked his Naval War Course students for encouragement and advice, and praised course director Captain Edmond Slade for his broad knowledge and support. Only then did he address fellow historians.[8] No previous British author had attempted a grand narrative driven by military theory on such a grand scale: This was British strategy in action—harmonizing political, diplomatic, naval, and military action—and it was designed to be read as a strategic template for the next conflict. Only a small leap of the imagination was required to replace Admiral Lord Anson's ships of the line with Fisher's dreadnoughts and Bourbon France with Hohenzollern Germany. Fisher loved the book, which placed maritime strategy at the heart of national policy. Little wonder the Army stopped inviting Corbett to its Staff College at Camberley: it had no answer to his scholarship, his intellect, or his argument.

The *Seven Years' War* appeared at the end of a critical year for Corbett: the first six months had been dominated by the three major essays and the last quarter by confidential work on an inquiry into the possibility of a German invasion of Britain. The inquiry had been urged by the Army, which hoped to prove invasion was possible and thus justify creating a greatly enlarged conscript army. Such proof would have weakened the Navy at the height of the arms race with Germany. Corbett had no difficulty demonstrating there was no historical or strategic basis for such concerns. These projects, which brought him into Fisher's Admiralty, debating with the Co-Efficients, and teaching at the Army Staff College Camberley marked a significant enhancement in the intellectual level of his work and established him as the most important contributor to the national debate and the obvious successor to Mahan.

By 1913 Corbett was lecturing from draft chapters of a "Confidential" history of the Russo-Japanese War that had been commissioned by the Committee of Imperial Defence. While Corbett stressed there was no correlation between past conflicts and future wars, he recognized his purpose was to equip officers to think about the present and future. He frequently posed the question "How would the various situations have been dealt with under present circumstances?"[9]

Teaching at the Army Staff College reinforced Corbett's argument that strategy must integrate all elements of national strength and not serve the agendas of individual armed forces. Unfortunately the British Army rejected joint planning, fearing the process would place it under naval direction. This response of the Army left the Royal Navy with no option but narrow naval planning. The Army's narrow-minded, self-interested obstructionism appalled Corbett and Fisher. Both men would devote their efforts to recovering the maritime basis of British national strategy. Corbett's objection was historical. Fisher had a more pressing agenda: he sought to subordinate the Army to the Navy in national strategy to facilitate defense economies. He wanted the Liberal government to reduce the Army rather than spread cuts across both Services. Recognizing an important ally in Corbett, Fisher skillfully deployed his work to shape the strategic debate in Britain and across the empire. Returning to the Admiralty in late 1914 Fisher based his war planning on the limited maritime strategy Corbett had laid out in the *Seven Years' War*.

Acutely aware that the relationship between history and strategy was a two-way process, Corbett, like Clausewitz, believed the interaction of evidence and argument was endless. Both men wrote histories as the testing ground for strategic ideas. Clausewitz considered generalized accounts of the past useless: "far better," he said, "to study one campaign in minute detail than to acquire vague knowledge of a dozen wars."[10] Critically, both Clausewitz and Corbett wrote their key theoretical works intended for officer education after sustained, nationally focused historical research. Clausewitz wrote for Prussians in the 1820s, Corbett for Edwardian Englishmen. Corbett's ability to develop French and German strategic ideas, dominated by military needs, into a British maritime form was exceptional.[11] His primary targets were not naval officers, who needed no convincing that British strategy was sea based, but rather statesmen and the soldiers who had fallen under the ghastly sway of late-nineteenth-century German military writers who corrupted Clausewitz into becoming an apostle of mass mobilization and "decisive" battle.

Corbett recognized that Britain needed a strong strategic doctrine in order to respond to challenges because the nation was not planning for a specific war or a specific opponent. These lessons apply to all Western democratic states in the twenty-first century.

Corbett exploited the theoretical writing of Clausewitz, Jomini, and the latest German analysts to take sea power theory beyond Mahan and other exponents of "naval" strategy.[12] His theoretical contribution included developing Clausewitz's limited/unlimited war dichotomy in the context of superior maritime powers operating against the offshore interests of continental powers. Such "offshore balancing" has been reinvented in the twenty-first century by strategists who sometimes appear unaware that Corbett had traversed the same ground a century earlier. *Some Principles* was a single-volume resume of the strategic doctrine intended to inform the defense of a global maritime empire—and it stressed deterrence above war. His core argument was that, while the principles of strategy were clear, their practical application at a national level was necessarily a unique cultural construction. British strategy was distinct from that of continental military nations, especially Imperial Germany, an argument intended to counter the conscriptionist and continentalist agenda of the British Army General Staff. A continental strategy was, Corbett argued, wholly antithetical to British interests and to Liberal politics.

With regard to the effective use of naval power, Corbett stressed the importance of doctrinal cohesion through a judicious combination of dispersed action and rapid concentration for battle. He considered Mahan's obsession with concentration unsuited to British needs. The Royal Navy needed a seamless, fluid movement between attack and defense, concentration and dispersal to meet and defend global shipping and an oceanic empire—something that was only possible with a powerful, coherent, and commonly understood doctrine—the sort that informed British cruiser operations in 1805. Today the Western world faces many of the same problems: British sea power has been replaced by the collective effort of many states, the United States and Britain prominent in their ranks, to secure the global commons and ensure the free flow of goods and services across the oceans. The world economy still depends on sea power.

Some Principles, written for the Committee of Imperial Defence, which needed a textbook dealing with national strategy for an enhanced Naval War and Staff Course, was the first primer about public national strategic doctrine, designed to inform decision making at the highest level and to integrate naval, military, and civil action to deter or if necessary wage war. *Some Principles* became a core text at the U.S. Naval War College. Corbett's friend Admiral William S. Sims, commander in chief of U.S. Naval Forces, Europe, volunteered to carry the second edition, which had been printed in Boston to meet American demand, to Britain on board an American warship because "[w]e have already benefited greatly by your advice and assistance in bringing to the attention of our Navy Department what ought to be done in this line."[13]

Sims' remarks demonstrate that Corbett had been central to the development and delivery of maritime strategy in the world's two largest navies before and during the First World War. He remains a major influence on both navies to this day, not the least because outstanding educators have ensured senior officers still have access to his ideas.

With the war course beginning to shape intellectual life of the Service Corbett's influence was central to the foundation of the *Naval Review*, a private circulation journal established in 1911 by war course staff, students, and alumni and led by Corbett's friend Captain Herbert Richmond. The *Review* advanced Corbett's mission to improve the standard of naval thought; it still provides a forum for Royal Navy officers to discuss strategy, tactics, and policy. The first editor of the *Review*, Admiral William Henderson, regularly sought his old friend Corbett's views on content. It is significant that his only essay in the *Review* addressed the importance of logical argument.

By 1912 Corbett's ambition had grown; he wanted to put naval history at the heart of the academic historical profession—not just in Britain but on the international stage. He aimed to generate additional war course textbooks on law, shipping, and tactics to support *Some Principles* and also his forthcoming strategic analysis of the Russo-Japanese War. This goal prompted a major methodological statement in his essay titled "Staff Histories," which he presented at the International Congress of Historical Studies in 1913. This work would be interrupted by the outbreak of war in August 1914.

When Britain went to war it applied Corbett's limited maritime strategy and provided an army to support continental allies. At this time the Committee of Imperial Defence hired Corbett to direct the Historical Section that would write the Official Histories. During the war Corbett produced important memoranda for "Jacky" Fisher; Maurice Hankey, the egregious and self-promoting secretary of the CID; and successive prime ministers; subjects were as diffuse as Baltic operations, the Dardanelles, and the conduct of Cabinet government. Corbett directed the collecting and processing of naval historical material and from 1916 compiled an Official History of Naval Operations, expressly modeled on his *Seven Years' War*, to ensure the war at sea was seen in the wider strategic context. He also supervised histories of the Merchant Marine, seaborne trade, and the war in the air. Predictably the Army took control of their Official History, producing turgid official accounts after the German model, piling up masses of tactical detail at the expense of accessibility, comprehension, and strategic insight.

Within weeks of the outbreak of war British politicians abdicated their long-established responsibility to provide the high-level direction of war. The Army exploited this opportunity to adopt a continental strategy, created the long-desired mass conscript army, and waged war at an unprecedented cost in lives and treasure. The soldier's brutal, attritional war destroyed the financial sinews and hard-won prestige that had sustained the British Empire for a century—the very result Fisher and Corbett had worked so hard to avoid. The soldier's war demonstrated the wisdom of Fisher's preference for deterrence and Corbett's limited war strategy. In June 1918 Corbett wrote to Fisher, the one man who truly valued his work. The letter contains a terrible, bleak message—one that should be read by every student of war and every author who ever thought their words could make a difference. It seemed the war would go on forever.

> I wept when I knew our whole Expeditionary Force was going to France, and felt what it would mean, and how Pitt [the Elder] would turn in his grave. Perhaps as Germany had got the initiative so completely, it could not be helped; but there is the cause of tears all the same. When the time came to strike amphibiously for a decision, we had nothing to

strike with. The first chance, as you saw, was at the Dardanelles, and once the decision obtained there we could have passed to the final one in the Baltic. Oh these blessed Germanised soldiers with their 'decisive theatre.' . . .

It is the most bigoted 'soldier's' war we have ever fought, and this at the end of all our experience. Why didn't I devote my life to writing comic opera, or collecting beetles? I might just as well. But now my fate is to tell the stupid story of the war as it is; not, alas, as it might have been. I had hoped when you came back, but already the soldiers had entangled us too far even for you to drag us out. We deserve each other's pity.[14]

Corbett and Fisher knew that their country had been blasted by a war that need not have been waged, and should not have been waged, in the way it was. Their work had been in vain—it had not been possible to turn insight and experience into policy and action. Fools, charlatans, soldiers, and politicians had thrown away a million lives, blasted many more, and wrecked the most successful economy in world history, opening a veritable Pandora's box of misery stretching from the influenza pandemic to genocide.

The loss of prestige and power left Britain vulnerable to the demands of other powers. The United States seemed determined to disarm sea power as a means of weakening British economic and political influence. In 1918 Corbett produced his pamphlet "The League of Nations and Freedom of the Seas," a crisp rebuttal of the American position, which was also aimed at a domestic audience that had missed the profoundly anti-British import of Woodrow Wilson's plans for a world peace that would serve the interests of one nation.

Two years into the First World War Corbett had the opportunity to develop his thinking about the role of naval history and the academic world in the development of naval thought, with an emphasis on strategy and doctrine. In his "The Revival of Naval History," a lecture in memory of the Sir John Knox Laughton, he stressed the need for specially trained academics to work with the Navy, using the university as the intellectual equivalent of a dockyard; and he discussed the unique and eccentric nature of the current conflict when contrasted with the preceding three hundred years of British strategic experience. The Navy would need historians solidly grounded in their discipline and specially trained to work on naval materials, to ensure they did not confuse the latest events with the ongoing realities of a unique national doctrine. The Professorial Chair in Naval History that he advocated was never created; however, the Department of War Studies, King's College London has sustained Laughton's pioneering work in the field down to the present.

In 1921, midway through writing an official history of the Great War that linked naval and strategic concerns, Corbett gave his last public lecture. He used the occasion to contrast British strategy in the revolutionary and Napoleonic wars with that of the recent conflict. He inferred that a limited maritime strategy that emphasized the fundamental importance of trade and merchant shipping, deployed a small volunteer army to secure British sea power, and waited for allies to carry their share of the burden of resisting pan-European hegemonic ambitions was both wiser and more appropriate. This strategic judgment was an obvious interpretation for the author of *Some Principles*, which had been so clear on the need for a national strategy that did not ape the continental dogma of contemporary German militarists. By advancing his case on the twin tracks of historical evidence and strategic theory, Corbett built a powerful intellectual edifice, one that has stood the test of time.

In the era when British defense policy was dominated by Cold War anxieties and a British Army on the Rhine, Corbett's work was criticized by the "Continental Commitment" school, khaki-clad cheerleaders for a major British military presence in Europe.[15] Fortunately the abrupt end of the Cold War consigned this relatively short-term strategic aberration to history. Modern Britain has never needed a mass conscript army because it has always been a sea power not a continental military state. Small insular states with limited manpower resources and fundamentally reliant upon global commerce and resource flows either prioritize sea power or perish. Today, neither military force nor land-based aviation can secure the seas on which such nations depend, any more than they could in Corbett's day.

Corbett had a sense of purpose, a mission. He dedicated his intellectual life to examining how Britain—his Britain, a global oceanic empire on a titanic scale—could be defended in the new century. His was a difficult task, hampered by those who feared that his enquiry, or his ideas, would damage their own interests—here small-minded soldiers and sailors share the blame with ignorant politicians. There was something heroic and tragic in the arc of Corbett's life; it was not the heroism of physical danger and personal risk but the heroism of a middle-aged man taking on a task that required more time and effort than he could hope to apply. His "defence studies" combined history, strategic theory, international law, education, and politics. It was all encompassing, rich, and above all national.

Corbett's insight and experience remain as pertinent today as they were in his own time. He stressed that the critical role of deep engagement with strategic history, examined at the level where civilian and military leaderships interact, was the basis for developing a clear concept of national strategy. To ensure this debate was open to all he provided a doctrinal template that situated national strategy in the wider theoretical debate about strategy. He ensured naval officers were equipped to debate strategy with their Army and civilian peers rather than continue assuming they had an unassailable case based on Admiral Lord Nelson, Trafalgar, and common sense. His opposition to the commitment of soldiers to continental conflicts in places that were not vital to the national interest will resonate with those who have had to live through the discretionary wars of the twenty-first century. Too many decisions were based on the interests of specific services, not nations or alliances.

The lesson for today is not so much what Corbett advised but the consequence of ignoring his advice. Between 1914 and 1918 the British managed to wreck a highly successful global position based on sea power and trade, suffering unprecedented human losses, incurring crippling debts, and taking on the burden of new responsibilities. In 1914 Britain was a creditor nation; by 1918 it was deeply in debt. Had Britain applied the same strategy to fight the Kaiser that it had when dealing with Napoleon, these outcomes might have been avoided. Corbett understood that national strategy had to balance vital interests, resources, and opportunities. He believed that Britain, a sea power, needed a maritime strategy led by the Navy. He knew that Germany, a continental power, needed a strategy led by the Army. Strategy is an applied art not a predictive science. By ignoring their strategic history, adopting an alien strategic model, and committing their manpower and resources to a continental conflict the British destroyed themselves. Little wonder Corbett despaired.

Despite the despair of 1918 Corbett never doubted it was his duty to persevere. He continued to engage with the biggest questions: Britain's place in the world and the existential threat it faced from those who would limit or abolish the ability to use sea control to impose economic warfare. Nor did he forget his core task, the strategic education of naval officers. We might read Julian Corbett's career as an intellectual triumph, but when he died in 1922 it must have seemed it had all been in vain. He could only hope his message and his books would make a difference the next time. Perhaps they did.

CHAPTER ONE

Defending the Admiralty and Disposing of Discontent

"Recent Attacks," Corbett's first major contribution to the naval policy debate in Edwardian Britain, needs to be read in context. Jacky Fisher's remarkable outburst of activity in the eighteen months that followed his elevation to First Sea Lord, the professional, naval head of the Royal Navy, had raised widespread opposition from many older officers. When Fisher was awarded a special promotion to admiral of the fleet, enabling him to remain in office for another five years, the opposition acquired a figurehead: as Fisher's promotion ended Admiral Lord Charles Beresford's hopes of reaching the top post, a "Syndicate of Discontent" assembled around him, with the intellectual content provided by Admiral Sir Reginald Custance, a more sophisticated officer who had fallen out with Fisher a few years earlier. The "Syndicate" was backed by retired admirals: the naval architect who built the "pre-*Dreadnought*" fleet, the Prince of Wales, and pro-Army elements in the Conservative Party. Using handpicked quotes from Captain Mahan, the opposition tried to derail Fisher's policies of strategic redistribution, all *Dreadnought*-type big-gun capital ships powered by turbines and submarines, along with the wholesale scrapping of obsolete warship tonnage, and the sale of obsolete stores. For many, the real problem was Fisher's decision to introduce a system of common entry for all new officers. By placing engineers

and Marines in the same stream as line officers, he under-
mined the social prestige of seamen and warfare officers over
that of engineers and Marines. While his object was efficiency,
Fisher took pleasure in applying a radical solution to a Service
over-blessed with titled admirals. He took his inspiration from
the American officer training system.

Corbett first came to Fisher's attention when he wrote in
defense of the educational reforms. The problem for Fisher
was a recent shift of political power that replaced Conservative prime minister Arthur Balfour, a convinced supporter,
with a new Liberal government that contained many economizing antimilitary radicals, including Winston Churchill and
David Lloyd George. Fisher needed to reach men who hardly
knew which end was the bow, and quickly, with an essay that
could explain Admiralty policy elegantly and economically.

The opportunity for Corbett and Fisher to respond came
late in 1906: the publication of a "Syndicate" essay by retired
admiral and navalist author Cyprian Bridge in the *Glasgow
Herald*[1] and the highly influential monthly journal *Nineteenth
Century and After*. Bridge lambasted the work of Fisher's tame
journalists: clearly something altogether more sophisticated
was required. As familiar with the world of journalism as that
of the Navy, Fisher secured a right of reply. He persuaded
Corbett to take on the challenge, demanded the editor give
him twenty pages, not fifteen, and offered the services of his
secretary and Captain Charles Ottley, the director of Naval
Intelligence, to assist the drafting. The essay would be an
"immense national service." Using Admiralty memoranda
Corbett quickly drafted the essay. Fisher edited the results,
commenting "Couldn't be better!"

The essay was classic Corbett: clear and direct yet subtle,
sophisticated, and propelled by conviction. He set up a debate
between individual examples of, on the one hand, self-
indulgent nitpicking by irresponsible critics and on the other
the coherent policy and strategy of the Admiralty. In the process he reduced the "Syndicate" to irrelevance, showing how

the entire program worked, with the mighty *Dreadnought* at its apogee. However, he did not expose Fisher's innermost thoughts, for those, as he knew, were even more radical and likely to generate more problems. Instead he carefully contrived the impression that "Syndicate" complaints were irresponsible, ill-informed, and unpatriotic. They had not demonstrated a superior policy but only attacked what was being done.

The essay was an instant success. Fisher's civilian superior, the First Lord, was "greatly impressed," as was the hitherto hostile Prince of Wales. Press opinion was equally enthusiastic. Fisher always reckoned the essay secured him an extra eighteen months in office. His reforms were secure, and the Navy moved forward into the twentieth century. Unlike the stable of supportive journalists that the old admiral managed, Corbett disagreed with aspects of Fisher's policy and did not disguise his views. Corbett was an early advocate for a modern staff and disliked the vindictive methods that were splitting the Service. Yet he knew there was no alternative. He knew Custance, the brightest of the "Syndicate," to be dogmatic, narrow-minded, and impervious to logical argument. In the short term there was no future without Fisher, but among the rising generation he had identified the coming men, among them John Jellicoe.

Corbett's essay demonstrated the importance of establishing a coherent naval message. Both he and Fisher recognized the difference between an in-Service debate, which could discuss major issues, and one conducted in the wider public, in which such exchanges would primarily diminish the standing of the Service vis-à-vis other services and reduce public and political confidence. The restricted, confidential *Naval Review*, to which Corbett stood as godfather, was the proper forum for serious debate. He recognized that the only beneficiaries of pieces like that published by Bridge would be the Army and the Treasury. Corbett did not agree with everything Fisher was doing and refused to support Fisher on some points, but he recognized that the Service must speak with one voice and have a coherent view of the Navy's place in strategy and policy. Petty quibbling over details should not be aired in the mainstream press. In such a free-for-all the most eloquent, not the most intelligent, might gain a hearing. The Navy needed a forum for debates about specific naval issues and a public voice for wider issues. The "Syndicate of Discontent" did enormous damage to the Navy between 1905 and 1910.

As if to emphasize his point, by late 1906 Corbett was hard at work on the evidence needed to demolish simplistic Army claims that invasion was a real danger. The same withering logic, mastery of evidence, and fluency of exposition that had won over the doubtful Liberal ministers and the wider public made short work of the simplistic case made by the soldiers.

RECENT ATTACKS ON THE ADMIRALTY

February 1907

Quiet people have recently become aware that there is in progress an agitation against the present Board of Admiralty of a very dangerous character. At first it was possible to ignore it as the ordinary well-meaning but misinformed criticism of men seriously interested in the welfare of the Navy. With scolding of this kind we are quite familiar, and we listen to it in the distance, if not with pleasure, at least with tolerance, as the index of a lively popular interest in the Service. It came from the usual sources which we know as well as the east wind and the fog, and there was no need for any man to leave his work to protest against ordinary climatic conditions. But lately the disturbance has begun to ring with a different sound. Statements and figures have been sown broadcast so recklessly untrue, to say no more, that they can no longer be accepted as candid criticism. And they have come, not only from the lower ranks of

---

Julian S. Corbett, "Recent Attacks on the Admiralty," *The Nineteenth Century and After,* February 1907, 195–208.

the Press, where the stress and hurry of early editions will excuse a good deal, but also from writers of a higher class who, at least, had leisure to weigh their words and test their allegations. To this has been added a flood of prejudice eagerly poured over every little untoward incident, such as are inevitable in the life of a great Service and are usually passed unnoticed. The rancour and bitterness with which such occasions have been seized are constantly increasing till, incredible as it may seem, we see a naval officer of high standing, and hitherto widely respected, being carried so far as to come perilously near to fomenting mutiny.

What does it all mean? We cannot tell. It is in any case needless to peer into the unsavoury background of which our senses make us painfully aware. For there is on the surface one plain meaning which concerns the very life of the country, and which the country should no longer endure.

For some years past a little band of men, whose services the country has never sufficiently recognised, had been awakening us by patient and persistent effort to what was meant by efficient naval administration and real preparedness for war. Some have been in the most honoured ranks of the Press and some in the Services, but all were of one mind. In season and out of season they preached the gospel of Von Moltke and the German Great General Staff and the possibility of adapting it to our own widely differing case. They taught us that the Navy needs a brain, that it needs direct responsibility each man for his own department—responsibility for war plans, for *personnel,* for material, for supply, and all that makes the active power of a great fleet. They have pointed out to us that the problem has never been solved except by a sound organisation which permits us to choose the right men and fit them in the right places to the best of our ability, and then without meddling to trust them to carry out our work and to hold them responsible if they fail. Above all, they have taught us that this method must apply in its strongest form to the man entrusted with plans of war. For plans of war imply secrecy—ultimately even secrets which must be locked in the breast of the war director alone—secrets which may involve his calling on his colleagues for measures and material which cannot fully be explained to them. In this way and for these reasons your man responsible for war plans must inevitably step into the position of the chief of the General Staff, and when that was done you would have a system under which efficient warfare and efficient preparation for war were possible. Every Commission that sat to consider the question more or less approximately endorsed these views. The country was at last converted and the whole Press took up the cry 'responsibility,' 'preparedness for war,' 'definite plans of operation.' The system was set on foot, the man was found, the thing began to move. Maybe it has not reached to so high a perfection as it will do some day ; but with the Sea Lords sitting a Board that is responsible for working the general policy, a First Sea Lord responsible for war plans, with a strong Intelligence Department assisted by the War College at Portsmouth, we have practically all the machinery of a true General Staff suited to our needs and methods.

Then what do we see? Under a masterful hand the machinery begins to move; war plans begin to shape themselves hand-in-hand with diplomacy, finance, and the Army; material begins to shape itself to war plans, and strategical disposition of the Fleet to both. Then incontinently, just as we are realising the good dream which we have dreamed so long, a crowd of little or anonymous men begin to cry an alarm, and demand that the machine shall be stopped and opened up for all the world to see what work it is doing. Such folly would be ludicrous were it not our own, and so full of peril. Can they not see? Amongst the loudest of the rioters are men who were the aptest pupils of those who led the good movement, and who a year ago were shouting most shrilly 'efficiency,' 'preparedness for war.' 'Moltke' and 'General Staff.' Did they really think that such a system could be worked without trust and without secrecy? Did they really think they could demand a full and categorical answer to every question their want of understanding or lack of information might suggest? Let them for a moment picture a band of journalists and unemployed officers cross-examining the German General Staff in the 'sixties.' Is it even thinkable? And yet the task for which Moltke had to prepare was simplicity beside the problems which confront the British Admiralty. Surely all those who are honest in the outcry have only to think a moment to see that no Staff system under heaven could work under such conditions. Already you have forced out information which as Englishmen you would not have sold to a foreigner for all he could give. And now when there is resistance, and you are answered according to your folly, you cry out that the country is being deceived, that the Admiralty is not to be trusted. Sir Alexander Cockburn, sitting in his place as Lord Chief Justice of England, once laid it down that there is no duty to tell the truth in answer to a question that a man had no right to ask. We may not care to adopt such a principle in civil life, but it is the essence of war. And if you find that in reply to one of your ill-judged demands you have received from the Admiralty less than the whole truth, for most of us it is a reason for trusting them more and not less. To deceive the enemy is a vital part of the work of a General Staff, and you too who hamper and thwart its work are the worst of enemies—for you are within our gates. Nor must you forget when Admiralty Memoranda are issued to satisfy your importunity, and you find them not guiltless of obscurity and even contradiction, that such memoranda are possibly not always intended entirely for home consumption.

This is especially the case where the disposition of the fleet is dealt with, and it is just here where the agitators are most active and the folly of their attitude most glaring. By events almost without parallel the whole political balance of the world has been upset. Europe itself has been metamorphosed almost as completely as it was on the eve of the Seven Years' War. The relations of the Powers are without precedent, and the Admiralty, in concert with the other Departments of State, has to work out from the beginning a disposition of the Fleet to meet the new and unexampled conditions. It is a work not only difficult, but requiring the utmost delicacy. The comity of nations demands that it shall be done decently. The bludgeon must not be flourished rudely in the face of sensitive neighbours with whom we have no quarrel and are on visiting terms. Let us see for a moment how the matter looks to them. In dealing with the reorganisation and redistribution of the Fleet in 1904 Admiral Baron von Maltzahn, one of the highest authorities on strategy in the German Navy, writes as follows:

> It is no longer a matter of 'preparation in peace for the approach of war.' . . . The British Fleet is actually ready for war and is drawn up against Europe. It only remains for it to take up the positions which have been arranged beforehand in the event of war. . . . Never have such measures been carried so far in time of armed peace.

These words, which cannot be denied, were written in January of last year. The attitude of which the Admiral complains has been in process of development ever since.

But this aspect of the situation—what we may call its political aspect—by no means exhausts its complexity. The same events which led to the political dislocation have also brought about a crisis in naval construction. For the first time since steam and iron and rifled guns began, fleets have been tested in a great naval war. We find ourselves suddenly in possession of a new point of view which should give us the means of distinguishing the false lines of development from the true, and enable us to stretch all the inchoate and half-seen elements of modern naval warfare to their logical conclusion. No Board of Admiralty ever had two such problems to grapple with at the same time. Every country is watching the other for a sign. One false step may have consequences beyond calculation. Is it too much to ask the tormentors to pause a moment and consider what a strain it means? Surely the most profound repose attainable on this earth is scarcely deep enough to permit the work being rightly done. Yet the Board of Admiralty, working under a tension almost beyond bearing, and toiling with ungrudging labour beyond all praise, must be assailed from day to day with every kind of interference these patriots can devise. Not a ship can be moved from one squadron to another without their crying that our supremacy is in danger, and demanding the reason why. They cannot wait for the laboriously formed plans to ripen in harmony with the material as it crystallises, and the policy as it solidifies. No! Because they have not the information or the understanding to see at once as far as the men who have been chosen and trained for the work, and who have all the threads in their hands: they cry out for cards to be thrown on the table that they may judge if the game is being rightly played. It is difficult to be patient with demands so preposterous. It is hard to believe that the mass of a people who have schooled half the world in the art of government have so little feeling for the elements of statesmanship. Surely they will not give a moment's hearing to such wanton impatience. Is it so hard to see in these movements the steady and harmonious development of a policy which shall ensure the peace of the world? Can ye not watch but one hour? What is still hidden from you is clear enough to those who most narrowly watch the new system. Here is an extract from an article upon it in the *Hamburger Nachrichten*, of the 1st of November last year. Speaking of the new Home Fleet, which is still in process of development, it says:

> The object is very plain. It shows an extraordinary carefully planned economy. For, just through this new organisation, a reduction of the Budget is attained, since a ship in the Reserve Fleet does not cost so much as one in the Active Fleet. We must, however, warn our readers against the deception which a number of English Conservative papers *bona or mala fide* give out, that the new organisation means a reduction of the English fighting force. Just the opposite is the case.

Those who have made a careful study of former wars or the preparations to prevent them—I do not mean merely from text-books, but those whose lot it has been to pore for many years over confidential State papers and to watch the development of such preparations in their inmost secrecy day by day, even hour by hour—will know that what the Hamburg paper says is solid truth. Such students, without any certain knowledge of what is in the mind of his Majesty's servants, will divine enough to see the general drift and pay homage to the astute and patient statesmanship with which the whole intricate game is being played.

If one who has devoted his life to the study of such matters in the past may say a word to his countrymen, it would be to trust a little longer the men to whom their chosen Ministers have committed the difficult work, and to shut their ears to the noisy 'experts.' Possibly many of these critics are really alarmed. Their tags of strategical lore, their 'instant readiness for war,' 'their principles of concentration,' and the like, imperfectly understood and usually misapplied, are quite enough to scare them. There is an old saying amongst lawyers that nothing is so misleading as a legal maxim. We may surely modify that. If a legal maxim misleads, a strategical maxim without the profoundest knowledge of its meaning is certain to trip you straight into the pit.

One word now, on the personal side of the question; for unhappily that side has been forced to the front too rudely to be ignored. These men who lately were demanding responsibility for plans of war, now that they have got it, are violently protesting against an alleged 'autocracy.' In tones of indignation and alarm they are crying out that the constitution of the Admiralty has been turned into a dictatorship; and to this they add a storm of detraction, which need not be noticed, against the man who is bearing the burden. Is their knowledge of human nature so small that they really believe it possible to find a man worthy of such responsibility who will not assert some kind of domination wherever he is? It is inherent in the personal element of the case, the personal element which, as all great strategists have taught, is the dominant force in war, and the solvent of all rule. It is a thing no plan of organisation can either create or prevent. Do they think they can toss out nature with a pitchfork, or bind the controlling factor in the art of war with a Departmental Minute? Men who can seriously advance such simple criticism are beyond argument. If Nelson were First Sea Lord they would call him a self-willed insubordinate poseur, as indeed he was at times. Or, if they had Drake he would be a vulgar bombastic fellow with no feeling for the traditions of the Service, which is also not entirely untrue. With such sorry lack of appreciation the country has nothing to do. All its concern is to see that it is well served, and who can say that it is not well served this day?

It will be asked, Is then no criticism of any kind to be permitted? Are the mouths of men genuinely interested in the Navy to be closed entirely? By no means. Not only is criticism to be permitted, it is to be encouraged, provided it be real criticism given with due regard to necessary limitations. It must be remembered that just as free States desiring the higher freedom of federation must each surrender part of its individual freedom, so where you wish to secure the working of a General Staff, and the free play of instructed opinion within its ranks, members of Parliament must forego a little of their right to question and the public dispense with part of its cherished privilege to carp and grumble. It is only the hasty, ill-considered persecution that is deprecated, for that is not criticism, it is irresponsible attack. All of it, or nearly all of it, is destructive ; none of it, or almost none, reveals any sympathy with the men who have to face the unprecedented difficulties of the time, or any real appreciation of the complex problem they are labouring to solve. The pity of it is great. For some at least of the men who are now sinning against their own creed most deeply have done in the past admirable work of the very kind that is wanted. They might well do it again, could they but rid themselves of the habit of critical tippling which has made them a prey to *hysteria navalis*. Constructive criticism, that displays a real desire to assist or even a moderate understanding of the problems at issue, is not likely to be ignored at the Admiralty. It is not the way with any Government Department, and no one who has a piece of honest advice to give need fear he will not be heard because he does not scream it from the house-top.

Again, it will be objected—if the General Staff system demands this self-restraint, this submission on the part of the public, what are we to do when we honestly believe the members of that staff are unequal to their task, are ruining the Navy and imperilling the country? Are we still to sit silent and passive? Again the answer is, By no means. There is open to you to use as freely as ever the constitutional means, which were employed in the case of Lord St. Vincent. The case against the Board should be presented to Parliament by the responsible leaders of the Opposition or, if the Opposition be content, by responsible and trusted men in the Government ranks. For this constitutional safeguard, this right of parliamentary inquiry which is so essential to the nation's trust in the Staff system, is an instrument of terrible power and danger. It is only to be wielded by the most experienced hands. Public opinion should forbid it to be so much as fingered by a recruit.

The Staff system rests on responsibility, and responsibility implies a free hand—free, that is, within the limit of our general policy. Without the one you cannot have the other. It follows you must trust your men or get rid of them. There is no third way. But to get rid of your men in the midst of their half-finished work, to change them for others practically pledged to undo it before ever they know fully the data on which the old men worked, is one of the most serious and responsible steps a popular Government can take. No man of any standing in the counsels of the nation would face it without the strongest provocation and the most overwhelming convictions. Yet every irresponsible assailant seems quite ready to rush in where statesmen fear to tread. It is always a hazard of the gravest land; it is triply a hazard in the midst of such a crisis in policy as that through which we are now passing. Once it was tried in the midst of war, and by no less a man than the younger Pitt; and in spite of his able leadership, the attempt, after causing incalculable hampering of the machine, recoiled with crushing force upon the heads of him and his colleagues. Now it is true we are not at war, but the situation demands no less undisturbed concentration of thought and work, and no less sustained continuity of policy. To change our team now while we are crossing waters, none the less deep because they are still, must certainly be full of peril, even if the new team proved better. The country should, with all its faith and fortitude, resist such a break; public opinion should sternly silence any agitation which seems to point that way—except on one condition. Nothing should permit such a change even to be considered, except overwhelming *prima facie* evidence that the trust they have given is misplaced.

Has such a case been made out? Will any man standing outside the controversy affirm it? Will anyone assert that, during the administration of the present head of the Naval Staff at the Admiralty, the Navy has not markedly increased in efficiency and readiness for war; that our sea-going fleets are not more numerous and better organised and disposed than they were; that their commanders were ever more wisely selected? Will anyone maintain that our Fleet was ever more efficient or relatively powerful than it is at this moment; that the *personnel* was ever more highly trained, whether in gunnery or in the higher spheres of tactics and strategy; that discipline and strenuous devotion to duty, whether in officers or men, were ever higher? History and living memory are clearly and absolutely against any such contention. Look abroad, and who will declare that our Fleet was ever regarded with more respect? All this is beyond contention, so far at least as a student may speak.

What, then, has the prosecution to set against this triumphant record? Now here we come to another class of critic which we have not yet noticed. If it were merely a question between the men who can show such a record of successful administration and the sufferers from *hysterianavalis*, the public need not hesitate to laugh the whole case out of court. But it is not so. The present administration is being attacked in the Press by a group of naval officers, of high rank and wide experience, who are either on half-pay or have reached an honoured retirement. They, too, are taking the same grave responsibility as their smaller allies, but it is to be assumed they are doing it deliberately from a pure sense of duty and no personal prejudice, and with a full apprehension of the risk to which they are pushing their country. The words of such men can only be treated with the respect they have earned, and their arguments should be seriously met. To attempt to do so in the compass of a short article is impossible—it would even be lacking in respect—for the indictment has been long and weighty and closely argued. Yet candour compels the expression of a clear opinion, and, so far again as an historian may speak without presumption—and they have called in history freely to their aid—the present writer would maintain, with all deference, that they have entirely failed to make out their case on any one line of their attack. And it is not without ground that historians may intervene. For, seeing how good the present is, the opponents of the Board are forced to look into the future, which they seem to do with genuine apprehension. To get a view forward they have to look back to history to trace the true direction of naval development out of the past, to project it into the future, and so to argue that our present policy is not proceeding on the right line. To history they have appealed, and by history let them be judged.

The main points on which the attack is being made are entry and training, dockyard policy, cruiser policy, big battleships, and fleet distribution. It is impossible to deal with them all. It must suffice to point out generally that the assailants are by no means at one on these points. In the eyes of some the present system of entry and training is the best work of the new school; with others it is ruinous. It is the same with the 'scrapping' of the small and early cruisers, the same with the economy in the dockyards; and while the admirals condemn the *Dreadnoughts*, the tremulous dram-drinkers cry continually for more. Let us take for consideration the two items with which the weightier criticism has dealt most fully—the cruiser and the battleship policies.

Let the cruiser case be taken first, for of all naval problems the future of the cruiser is the most difficult. Beside it the question of the battleship is simple and certain. The charge against the Board—so far as the charge can be formulated from its many inconsistent presentations—is that it has departed from an alleged tradition of naval warfare which differentiated sharply between the cruiser and the battleship type; that, ignorant (so it is frankly said) of the elementary principles of naval warfare, our sea lords have exhibited a tendency to suppress all small cruisers and create in their room a type of vessel which closely approximates to the battleship; and that, contrary to all precedent, they are more and more regarding these cruisers as part of our battle strength, and that it is consequently becoming impossible to detach them for cruiser work without sinning against the strategical rule of keeping your battle squadrons concentrated. It is further said that as a result of this policy of costly large cruisers, our cruisers cannot be numerous enough for our needs. From the roving and contradictory manner in which this charge is formulated, it is difficult to know whether one has done it justice. For instance, the two ablest writers base their attack on mutually destructive reasons. One condemns the armoured cruiser because for fleet work all its advantages could be obtained by detaching fast battleships to support cruisers of the older type; and the other because the system of armoured cruisers entails detaching part of your battle force for cruiser work. Such contradictions are common and confusing. Still it is hoped the above is a fair presentation of the indictment.

The clearest and most weighty statement of the case for the prosecution appears in a very recent article by one of the distinguished officers above referred to, who throughout has shown himself the ablest and most independent and genuinely reasonable of the opposition. After his scholarly method, he has approached the question from the historical point of view. In a most able and exhaustive manner he has traced the development of the cruiser from Elizabethan times, with the object of showing—unless we mistake him—that there exists this principle in naval warfare which demands a marked differentiation between cruisers and battleships; that all intermediate types are false; and that, whatever our adversaries do, we should cling to the policy of numerous and cheap and comparatively small cruisers.

Learnedly as the case is presented, it is not convincing. It leaves room to doubt whether the story leads quite surely to such a conclusion. As set forth by his careful pen, it seems to tell that all through the days of our sailing fleets we never did differentiate sharply between the two types except once when we followed the French. The logical unsoundness of intermediate types was periodically felt, and yet, in practice, some unformulated exigencies were perpetually compelling us to recur to those types. The point is of high interest and well worth thorough investigation. For the moment, however, the question is different. The graver question is whether the whole of this history is not out of court. A naval historian is the last person in the world to belittle the value of naval history in clearing questions of to-day, but he cannot deny how misleading history may be if we look for guidance on the surface instead of seeking the underlying conditions which give that surface its conformation. The value of history is not only to set forth the experience of the past, but also to show when some radical change of fundamental conditions has made that experience dangerous precedent. Now it is not difficult to show that within the last few years such a fundamental change has taken place in the conditions of the cruiser problem. This change the Board of Admiralty seems to have recognised with fine penetration while the rest of us were raking the surface.

The main functions of cruisers are twofold—to act as the eyes or screen for a fleet and to destroy or protect commerce. There are of course subsidiary uses for small cruisers, such as inshore work amongst mine-fields, or in combined expeditions, and so forth ; but for such work cruisers are not absolutely indispensable. It is the two main and essential functions that must control the type. In both spheres the fundamental conditions of their work have been turned upside down since the era of wooden sailing fleets. In those days it may be broadly stated that after a certain mean was passed the larger a ship was the lower its sea-speed and what the Elizabethans called its 'nimbleness.' To-day the reverse is the fact. The larger a ship is now, by the same broad rule, the higher is its sea-speed, while its 'nimbleness' is practically unaffected. The consequences go to the root of the whole question. In the old days a frigate could lie to windward of an enemy's fleet for days in perfect security, knowing that nothing could touch her or shake her off except superior force of her own class. But in these days of fast battleships such work is impossible to small or even middle-sized vessels. For if you give them the speed to escape you must deprive them of the mobile endurance to sustain their watch. Again, in the sphere of commerce. In the old days a frigate could always overhaul the finest types of merchantmen, like the East and West Indiamen and the galleons of Spain ; and if one cruiser was too small to deal with them two could be coupled. Now all this is changed. The great liners of to-day have nothing to fear from any ship or group of ships corresponding in military value with the old frigate.

They can outrun them and outstay them. Nor is it merely a question of destroying an enemy's commerce. It is also one of protecting our own. Should such liners be equipped as commerce-destroyers, with their high and sure seaspeed and their enormous storage capacity for coal, how are they to be dealt with by small cruisers?

Here, in these changed conditions, lies the thorniest question of naval policy. How is it to be answered? How are we to steer in this uncharted sea? Clearly there is no salvation in small cruisers. No multiplication of them will compensate for their low sea-speed and small endurance. These qualities can only be obtained in cruisers of the largest size. Shall we then trust to our own merchant liners for the work? They would serve admirably for the eyes of a fleet, but without any considerable fighting power they could not serve as a screen, for they could not drive in the cruisers of the enemy. For dealing with enemy's commerce-destroyers no certain reliance could be placed upon them, and at the same time their removal from their true sphere must cause a grave disturbance of trade. Shall we then seek a solution in large protected cruisers? The idea commends itself to no one. Some years ago, it is true, France built one or two such ships; but she has not repeated the type, and no first-class naval power has followed her lead. The truth is such ships are very costly in men and money, and are of low fighting power in proportion to their cost. By spending a little more in giving them armour you get a vessel with almost all their qualities, costing no more for upkeep, and of high fighting value. But here comes in the objection that every time you detach them from your fleet you diminish its fighting power. It is a real objection, though by no means so great as it was before the recent rapid development of wireless telegraphy. Still it raises the question whether some smaller type of fleet cruiser could not be devised which would greatly diminish the number of occasions for detaching armoured cruisers—some development or variant perhaps of the scout type which for cruiser work in war would fill the gap between destroyers and armoured cruisers, and in peace time discharge the police duties of the Navy.

Such, roughly stated, is the complex equation that has to be solved. It is one of extraordinary difficulty that no Admiralty yet sees its way through. For no country are the factors more complicated than in our own case, and it is the duty of every patriot, if he cannot assist the solution, to refrain at least from increasing the difficulties of the Board by raising matters of prejudice. The solution will not be helped by intemperate talk about 'scrapping' ships whose *raison d'etre* has gone with the advent of new conditions. It is objected that Admiral Togo found such types useful. It is not said in the same breath, as it should be, that he was acting against a battle fleet of the old slow type. Nor are those days recalled—days of terrible anxiety and peril through which he had to pass at the zenith of the crisis, simply because he could not throw such weak cruisers as far forward as the strategical dilemma demanded. Nor, again, is it any help to assert that armoured cruisers were a failure in the late war. Such a statement cannot be supported on the evidence, at least so far as it is available. In any case it is a serious responsibility to make such a statement without at the same time pointing out that the Japanese themselves are not of this opinion. They, with all their experience, are now building six cruisers. Five of these are armoured vessels of about 14,000 tons, and one is of the older type of 4,000.

The question of the big, one-calibre, high-speed battleship requires similar treatment, but space will not permit. It may, however, be pointed out, that here again the historical argument is misleading. The able officer already cited has sought to show, in tracing the development of the capital ship, that increase in size gives no superior battle strength, because there is a law of 'equality,' which always comes in, compelling your adversary to increase the size also, and leaving you in the same relative position as before. The net result, in consequence, is that you either increase the cost of naval defence or diminish the number of your units. Yet his careful study of the process reveals clearly that line-of-battle ships, and indeed, frigates, did go on increasing in size till the end of the period. How is this to be accounted for? Were our constructors, and those who controlled them, from first to last all as misguided as the present Board is alleged to be? Surely not. The explanation is that the story, as the distinguished officer tells it, reveals another law, the law of 'inequality' or 'over-trumping.' His candid statement of the facts tells us, in spite of himself, that this is a law as overbearing and certain in its action as the law of 'equality.' We, and the French, have been mainly responsible for it. We have played the game over and over again, but never with results more disturbing to our neighbours, or more comfortable for ourselves, than when we put down the *Dreadnought*. The card has been well and boldly played, but none the less is it certain that the old law was forcing the hands that played it. Whether we are conscious of it or not, it is a law of unyielding power—no more to be resisted by our present Board than it was by the great naval first lords of the eighteenth century. No matter how the Exchequer may complain, the law will go on working like the tide till a point is reached when it is proved beyond a shadow of doubt that increase of size no longer increases fighting value, or till some consideration of material bars further growth.

Now for some time past we have been listening to a very earnest contention that this dead point, at least so far as fighting power is concerned, has been passed in the *Dreadnought* design. The arguments in favour of this view have been ably presented, amongst others, by Captain Mahan in America, and by scarcely less respectable authorities in this country, in France, and in Italy. Yet the fact remains that they have entirely failed to convince the Admiralty Staffs of any naval power. The tactical advantage of a shortened line, and to some extent of high speed, the facility of fire-control, the increased protection for guns and gun-crews, and the higher power of hitting which this type secures overweigh all the argument of the accomplished opposition. It is never pleasant to find that the theorists and the practical men are not at one. To serious people it must bring a sense of uneasiness and anxiety. But in this case there seems to be a clear explanation. It is that the theorists are once again arguing on the surface, while active men have probed to the bed-rock. The use of naval tactics is to enable you to hit your enemy more often and more severely than he can hit you. The theorists count up the weight of metal that a ship of the old type can deliver and find it is greater than that of the new. For them this settles the matter. The practical men, however, count the hits as demonstrated in battle practice, and find that for reasons well known to the gunnery staff, the advantage is distinctly on the side of the one-calibre 12-inch type. And beyond this there is the additional accuracy and sustenance of fire due to the fact that undeniably in the new type the gun-crews can be protected to an extent that was impossible in the old.

In combating the advantage of the shortened line, it must be said, with great reluctance, that some of the opposition seem for a moment to have lost their grip of the theory they advance. They argue that the massing of guns in a few big ships is contrary to the great military principle that you should distribute your guns and concentrate your fire. Now the preoccupation of every admiral in command of a long line is to manoeuvre it as tightly closed up as he dare. He is fighting instinctively all the time against the principle of distribution. The fact is that what is meant by distribution ashore is something radically different from ranging your batteries as close together as you can in one line. It means separating them as widely as possible so as to secure the most disturbing cross-fire. We cannot but unwillingly admit that the respected authorities who have advanced this argument have stumbled over a strategical maxim which they have not paused to analyse. The fact is that it will not apply to the naval line of battle, and so far as it is applicable to sea warfare at all, it is an argument, not for numerous small ships, but for breaking up your fleet into free-acting groups or divisions.

That such arguments have been set forth by serious authority is unfortunate. It is just the kind of reasoning that makes practical men impatient of theory. Yet the arguments come from the very men who have done most to persuade naval officers how much there is to be learnt from theory and history. Indeed, we can read beneath all they write on these points, and they even have at times openly said so, that the effect of the new school will be to make the Service rely on material rather than upon the sagacious study of tactics and strategy and the whole art of war. That apprehension deserves all sympathy, and honours those who feel it. But is there—in our Service at least—any ground for it? In any case, it is certain that during the reign of the new school the desire to see the art of war studied methodically, which the salt of the Service has so long striven for, has been pushed steadily forward to a point it has never attained before. It is also true that the very men who are most closely and deeply engaged in these studies are just those who are most securely convinced of the practical and theoretical correctness of the one-calibre big battleship.

Of the charge which is most loudly brought against the Admiralty and the Government, that they are letting our standard of naval power fall below the safety limit, nothing has been said. The fact is that the charge is quite untenable—it has not been supported by any journal of first-class standing, nor by any writer of weight, no matter how great and genuine his mistrust of the present Board. Nor can any such indictment be drawn, except by taking all that it is said that foreign nations say they are going to do as done or nearly done, and crediting our own administrators with every quality which they have fully demonstrated they do not possess. There is no case, and they know there is none. Hence the sporadic cry for 'inquiries.' In the Temple they know the device well as an attorney's trick to extract facts on which to found a case. They call them 'fishing interrogatories.' It is a sport which judges severely repress. Let public opinion severely do the same. Such inquiries, even when well founded on a decent *prima facie* case, are serious evils, in that they interrupt work, distract the office concerned, and end, if they end in anything, in our overworked administrators consenting to some compromise, wholly indefensible on any theory, in order to rid themselves of the annoyance and get to honest work again. In the present case it could only end, as it did in Lord St. Vincent's case, by proving that the very points on which he was most acrimoniously attacked were just those on which he had deserved best of his country and the Service.

For all of us there are points in the present policy with which we do not agree, or, to put it more modestly, of which we do not understand the meaning. But which of us has so much confidence in his judgment upon such matters as in self-communing solitude to assure himself such doubts are grounds for an inquiry? Of course there are many whose deep interest in the Navy fills them with a craving to know, but are they really ready to answer to the country for stopping the machine at this moment and inevitably revealing matters of priceless value to our competitors, gratuitously, which nothing could bribe them to disclose? For this—and let there be no mistake—this is what inquiry means. Seriously, is it not time to stop, as a high national duty, before further harm is done, and we become a laughing-stock to the world?

CHAPTER TWO

Defending the Dreadnought

Fisher was equally taken with Corbett's next article, "The Strategical Value of Speed." Alongside the general criticism of Admiralty policy, addressed in "Recent Attacks," naval opinion was deeply divided over the wisdom of the new capital ships—Fisher's epochal battleship HMS *Dreadnought*, and HMS *Invincible*, later classified as a battle cruiser. The new ships combined an all-big-gun armament, large size, and high speed with consequently increased costs. Many naval officers doubted the wisdom of the move, among them Mahan, who would debate the subject with William Sims in the United States. In Britain the leading exponent of the small, moderate-speed battleship was Admiral Sir Reginald Custance. His articles, published under the transparent pen name "Barfleur," the name of a small battleship he had commanded, had been reprinted in the book *Naval Policy* in 1907. Corbett's copy contains marginalia that relate to this paper and "Recent Attacks." Although Corbett had worked closely with Custance on the history of tactics and signalling, and had been appointed to teach on the Naval War Course at Custance's suggestion, he found himself obliged to disagree profoundly with the admiral. In his view it was high time the Navy was taught to think as rigorously as it exercised at great guns.

This time Corbett chose to address the naval professional audience head-on, speaking at the Royal United Services Institute, the leading British defense forum. The prestigious

building on Whitehall was normally the platform for flag officers and field marshals, not cultured literary or academic
types. Yet, for all the diffidence with which he opened his argument to an audience dominated by senior naval officers—and
omitted the name "Barfleur" from his paper entirely—the cri-
tique was unsparing. He began by attacking the method and
coherence of Custance's argument, a relatively easy target. He
deployed a recent French essay to highlight the proper
approach, using an argument based on logic rather than
examples handpicked to sustain the thesis. He demonstrated
that Britain's advantageous global position was best served by
big, fast ships. Then he countered Custance's selective use of
history with far stronger examples. He deployed the highly
esteemed Admiral Sir Thomas Hardy, Nelson's right-hand
man, as a proto Fisher First Sea Lord. As First Sea Lord
between 1830 to 1834 Hardy had built big battleships and
scrapped small, obsolete types. He also added detail from
Admiral Kempenfeldt's writings, which demonstrated the vital
role of speed in defensive warfare.

In this article Corbett developed key lines of argument
that would reach fruition later in *Some Principles*, including the
importance of clear argument and the avoidance of simplistic
dogma and special cases. He dissected the contemporary
obsession with "offensive" warfare, a shibboleth almost as
prevalent among sea officers as among soldiers, emphasising
that it had always been necessary to defend in some areas, to
amass forces and attack in others. He did not excuse Mahan
in this respect but emphasized that many of the more extreme
arguments flowed from a somewhat loose reading of the great
man's works. Corbett also linked the paper to his examination
of economic warfare, emphasising how "torpedoes, wireless
telegraphy and submarines" had changed the strategic situation and ended the old close blockade system. These insights
reflected his 1906 work on the conceptual element of Admiralty War Plans; he also laid out the germ of the British open
or distant blockade of 1914 and linked it to speed.

The discussion that followed the paper indicated that most senior officers accepted Corbett's methodological arguments and agreed with his conclusions and, by extension, those of "Jacky" Fisher on speed and the *Dreadnought*. Yet, they remained unhappy about the mass scrapping of obsolete tonnage. Corbett admitted that "Barfleur" had been his target and extended his discussion to include the tactical perspective. While Custance argued a faster fleet could be countered by turning away, Corbett observed that simply turning the enemy off course could be a major strategic achievement. He concluded by stressing the distinctive spheres of expertise of the historian and officer and the relative merits of historical examples and recent experience. Mahan did not choose to reprint this essay.

A week later Corbett was lecturing to the Naval War Course in Portsmouth. In June 1908 Fisher solicited another essay in defense of the *Dreadnought*. Corbett, who had lost many naval friends by so openly espousing Fisher's cause, did not oblige.

At the time Corbett was writing, the cult of the offensive had gripped the minds of continental strategists. German and French war plans envisaged massive strategic offensive operations into hostile territory to secure a "decisive" battle and settle the war. The result was the "Schlieffen" Plan of 1914 and the French Plan XVII. Both were catastrophic failures. The attempt to secure politico-strategic victory by outsized tactical thought ignored Clausewitz's dictum on the superior strength of the defensive. Corbett had a far more sophisticated approach to Clausewitz: he objected to the intellectually dishonest attempt to simply transfer the lessons of land warfare into naval operations and to the absolutely perverse misreading of British naval history, in which Fisher's critics argued that "decisive" victories had been secured by offensive operations. By exercising command of the sea and defying the enemy to challenge that command, the Royal Navy could conduct blockade and offensive operations from a strong defensive position. In 1914–1918 the Grand Fleet at Scapa Flow covered the rest of the world ocean, where Britain conducted many strategic offensives. The German High Seas Fleet could challenge that command only by steaming to Scapa, but Scapa was too far away for the Germans to bring most of their torpedo boats and destroyers.

Modern western navies, familiar with the easy command of the seas common in most post-1945 conflicts, need to reflect on the challenges faced off the Falkland Islands in 1982 and the more serious prospects of a more nearly symmetrical threat at sea. Corbett's insight offers some useful pointers from an age when the combination of rapidly developing technologies and evenly matched fleets obliged strategists to begin with securing command—a primary concern that might affect the balance of assets.

THE STRATEGICAL VALUE OF SPEED
IN BATTLESHIPS

March 1907

I feel that in approaching a subject on which so wide a difference of opinion exists amongst distinguished officers, not only in this country, but in all countries, some kind of apology is necessary from a civilian. I want, above all, to disclaim the idea even of attempting any dogmatic conclusion on the subject. I do not think it is possible for any one in my position to do more than endeavour to point out where argument seems to have gone astray in this discussion, and to point out certain lines of argument which appear to be unsound, and certain fallacies which tend to recur in all discussions of this kind. I felt it might be possible perhaps to assist by indicating where such false lines of argument and fallacies

Julian S. Corbett, "The Strategical Value of Speed," *Journal of the Royal United Services Institute,* July 1907, 824–39. Paper delivered June 3, 1907.

have come in, with the hope of discovering why it is that these remarkable differences of opinion exist, and also how we can best get rid of them.

I will commence with an attempt to state what the problem really is, in order to arrive at what the true line of argument should be. It is extremely important to do this, although I believe it to be an Anglo-Saxon failing almost always to approach a discussion without first having stated as clearly as possible the proposition that is going to be discussed. We are all of us inclined to do that, and the result is that we find ourselves going into a number of partial arguments which deal with only part of the case, or else are entirely off the line.

Now, in none of our British or American writers, so far as my knowledge of the controversy goes, have I found such a statement, but the moment we turn to the French writers we find it laid down quite clearly. I will take as an instance the author who writes under the pseudonym of "Michel Merys," who is a *lieutenant de vaisseau* in the French Navy, and may be classed as an opponent of high speed. In seeking to reach a real statement of the case, he begins by eliminating from the discussion the main point on which we all agree and he starts with this postulate: that the strategical value of high speed, considered alone, independently of its reactions, is beyond doubt. I think that is a proposition on which everyone is agreed. He then considers the reactions. He tells us that they are both tactical and strategical. The tactical reactions mean that high speed is apt to lower the capacity of a ship for gun power, armour, and the like. With these tactical reactions I do not propose to deal, as they are beyond my power, and the present purpose. I wish merely to direct your attention to the strategical reactions—the strategical reaction, I may say, for there is only one main reaction, which Merys calls the radius of action. In other words, the strategical reaction of high speed is that it tends to a diminution of the radius of action owing mainly to increased coal consumption.

I use that old expression, "radius of action," although others have been suggested recently. I doubt whether they really help the matter. We have "Mobile endurance," "Enduring mobility," "Coal endurance," and such-like expressions, but I think "Endurance" is really all that we require—"endurance," or the old term, "radius of action."

Now, in approaching this question we ought to know whether radius of action falls in proportion to the rise of speed. Whether that has ever been ascertained accurately I cannot say, but it is wise, for the sake of our discussion to-day, to assume that it does; and we will, therefore, assume that gain in speed is always balanced by a proportional loss in endurance. When we have admitted that we are in a position to get a fairly clear statement of the question. It is this: Has speed or radius of action the higher strategical value? Or, as the French authority puts it: "Which of the two lends itself to the greater number of strategical combinations?" That is the vital question as to the strategical co-efficient of speed. There is, it is true, another which relates to the number of units. Increased speed tends to increase the size of the ship, and, consequently, to diminish the number of units. That is also a strategical question, but we will omit it, at all events for the present, because it is really so much more bound up in the question of big ships than in the question of speed.

Now let us see how English writers approach this question; I mean how our recent writers, of what I may call the moderate speed school, have approached the solution of the question. At the outset I do not think we can help noticing a marked tendency to cite cases where radius of action is clearly more important than speed, and to ignore all others. Here we have the first erroneous line of argument, this tendency to quote cases that deal clearly in one direction and to ignore all the others. Such a method does not help us at all, because each case that is cited can be met, in all probability, by a case where speed is distinctly more important than radius of action, and we get no further. You will notice in all these writers that practically all the cases they cite are cases of wide oceanic movements.

Contrast this method with that of the French authority. He sees at once that his proposition is not necessarily true in all cases. He sees there is a wide logical difference between the case of oceanic movements and the case of movements in narrow seas. Therefore, he distinctly says that his proposition with regard to the higher value of radius of action is only true for what he calls *les grandes traversees*, or wide oceanic movements, and he cites the cases of the voyages of Rodjestvensky in the Russo-Japanese War, and Cervera in the American-Spanish

War. He does not even attempt to contend that his proposition is true of operations in narrow seas. He admits that narrow seas are an exception to his rule.

Now, having pointed out the way the French officer approaches the subject, distinctly seeing the difference between oceanic operations and operations in narrow seas, let us examine more closely the way in which British officers approach it. I will quote one, perhaps the ablest, certainly the most persuasive advocate of moderate speed. In advocating radius of action above high speed he maintains that his view is supported by history, and having said that, he proceeds to justify his claim by quoting the case of Villeneuve chased by Nelson and Rodjestvensky's voyage. Without wishing to pre-judge the case in any way, I should like to submit to you that that kind of argument cannot be passed.

To support his assertion that history is on his side, he quotes two cases, both of which are absolutely without precedent in naval warfare. Not only are they without precedent, but they are both oceanic. One cannot help noticing again—I hope I may say it with great respect merely as the view of a civilian—a tendency in service discussions to found arguments on exceptional cases because they are at once the most conspicuous, the most brilliant, and the best known.

I notice that, not in a carping spirit, but as a warning against the danger. The thing that really counts, above all, in strategy is the forgotten, humdrum, every-day normal, not the brilliant exceptions; and to say that naval history is on your side because Nelson's chase of Villeneuve, or Rodjestvensky's voyage, appear to tell in your favour, is argument upon which it is not safe to rely. In this case the distinguished officer not only entirely ignores the normal, but he also fails to draw the French lieutenant's distinction between oceanic operations and those in narrow seas. If he had wished to complete his argument, after dealing with two oceanic cases, he ought at once to have dealt with two operations in narrow seas.

So much for the arguments which are logical and those which are not. Now let us admit the logical arguments for moderate speed, and see where we arrive. Well, we get to this point, that in oceanic movements, endurance is more important for strategical combinations than high speed. I do not mean to say that that is quite certain, but it is well, at all events for the present, to admit it for the sake of eliminating differences and simplifying the discussion. Therefore, let us admit that. At the same time, we have to take the position that it is not true for narrow seas; that is to say, it has not been proved. For while some critics do not even attempt to prove that high speed is not of greater strategical value for narrow seas, the rest of them admit that it is of greater strategical value in narrow seas. Therefore, we must assume that high speed is of greater value in narrow seas until we get at least a *prima facie* case that it is not.

But the case is not completely stated even yet. We want to know whether this proposition of Merys's is true for all Powers. Strategical conditions, and the function of the fleet, differ very greatly according to the geographical conformation and distribution of various states, and to their international characteristics. Let us take our own country, and let us ask what is the main function of our fleet? I think we must answer that the main function of our fleet is to control the "Narrow Seas," and there-fore, *prima facie,* that its main strategical interest lies in high speed rather than in endurance, certainly as to that part of the fleet which is intended for home defence. I feel that that statement of the function of the fleet is liable to be disputed, but I am quite prepared to maintain, though there is no time to do it now, were it disputed, that undoubtedly, from the point of view of scientific strategy, the control of home waters is beyond shadow of doubt the primary function of our fleet.

Now, as to the rest, imperial and commercial defence, how does it work out? Admitting that radius of action is the important thing in this case, where the operations are largely oceanic, we get this proposition, that the difficulty of the British task in imperial and commercial defence is in proportion to the radius of action possessed by the enemy's ships. It would seem, therefore, that in this case we ought to go rather for radius of action than for high speed. But in oceanic warfare, endurance, radius of action, does not depend entirely on coal capacity; it depends also for practical purposes on coaling supply and coaling stations. Our foreign authorities notice this and proceed to destroy the whole of their argu-ment, so far as we are concerned, by admitting that for us radius of action is less vital than it is for them, owing to the number and disposi-tion of our coaling stations.

What follows from this? If we force our rivals to sacrifice endurance to speed, the easier is our Imperial defence. By a policy of high speed we involve them in a strategical dilemma. They must either increase their speed so as to equal us in the vital area of our home waters, and so render our Imperial defence easy by reducing their radius of action; or they must sacrifice their position at home and contend with us in the oceanic areas, where we are particularly strong in coal supply, and able thereby to a great extent to neutralise their assumed superiority in radius of action. That dilemma seems to me inevitable so long as we go in for high speed. Now, the only escape from that—there is an escape, but only one—is for our rivals to follow us in building big ships, which combine speed and radius of action. That is our policy today? Is it wise?

Here I would beg to say a few words on this subject of big ships, because the whole question of the strategical value of speed tends to lose itself ultimately in the Question of big ships. It is well to approach such a subject by asking two questions. The first question is: What is the tradition of the service? The second question is: What, theoretically, is the strategical effect?

What then, firstly, is the tradition of the service about big ships? If we turn to the highest authorities, who recently have dealt with this point, we find one of the best of them saying that in adopting this policy of very powerful big ships, "the experience of generations of seamen has been discarded and declared to be wrong."

I venture to differ from that entirely. It is a question of history, and I hope I may differ without presumption from the distinguished officers who have held that point of view. I will not rely upon my own interpretation of history: I would rather call witnesses. In the whole roll of the great seamen of our Navy, there is no greater name on such a point than Sir Thomas Hardy, Nelson's Flag-Captain. It will be remembered that it was of Sir Thomas Hardy, Nelson said: "I never knew Hardy wrong on any professional subject; he seems imbued with an instinctive right judgment." Hardy, in 1830, became First Sea-Lord, and, I believe, he is handed down in the traditions of the Admiralty as one of the best that was ever there. At that time, owing to the demoralising effect of a continued and undisputed command of the sea, we were going in for swarms of small cruisers and seventy-fours as ships of the line. Hardy, when he came to the Admiralty, laid it down as his guiding principle that it was powerful ships of the line which carried everything in a general action, and that it was large frigates which disposed of the smaller craft. I give you that on the authority of Sir John Briggs, in his work on "Naval Administrations." Sir John Briggs knew Hardy well. When he got to the Admiralty he immediately set about laying down a programme for three-decked ships only; he cut down the seventy-fours into 50-gun frigates, the 46-gun frigates into corvettes, and he struck from the list the whole of the small cruisers, or nearly all of them; that is to say, all the "donkey" frigates, as they were called then, and all the sloops and "coffin" brigs. That I would remind you is really the last word of the Nelson school, the last word of the sailing admirals, for it was also Hardy who introduced steam into the fleet.

When such a man does such a thing as that, we ought to be very careful in saying of recent policy that it betrays a want of knowledge and want of study of the art of war. I do not think any one would dare to say that of Sir Thomas Hardy, and Sir Thomas Hardy was clearly of opinion that big battle-ships were the ships that carried everything before them in a general action, and that large frigates disposed of the smaller craft. I do not say that that proves everything for us now, but it does prove that we ought to be very careful how we talk about the traditions of the service without having studied what the tradition of the service was throughout the whole period of which we are speaking.

Now let us leave that and ask our second question: What is the strategical effect, theoretically, of big ships, for us? Big ships, as we see, are entailed by an effort to combine high speed and radius of action. I venture to put it to you that big ships in themselves are strategically favourable to us because theoretically they are favourable to the power which has the best harbours. It means that if we have a number of deep water harbours, and our rivals have little more than tidal or shallow harbours, our strategical positions are better and more numerous than those of our enemy. On this account, therefore, that is, from the point of view of big ships as well as from the point of view of our wealth in coaling stations along the ocean routes, a policy of high speed seems to be distinctly one method of improving our geographical conditions.

It is to this point we seem to come by a process of purely theoretical argument. The conclusion may, of course, be wrong. All I desire to assert is, that the line of argument I have tried to indicate is one that has been neglected and one which really ought to be worked out by competent authority. I feel very strongly that on such a subject as this an open mind and strict impartiality are absolutely necessary. I know that the argument, as I give it, must appear hostile to those who have opposed high speed. That is not from any feeling of hostility. It is merely a logical necessity, because the onus of proof is on them. They have raised a question of the greatest importance. There is no doubt that we were all inclined to take the value of high speed a little too much for granted. They have undoubtedly done great good in raising this question, but in doing so they are challenging the wisdom of an old tradition, and they must accept the burden of proof. Consequently, in testing their arguments, we are bound to take the attitude that they have not proved their case. The tradition of the service has undoubtedly been, so far as I can understand it, ever since Elizabethan days, towards getting the utmost possible speed in battle-ships, and great sacrifices of fighting strength have constantly been made for it. That is too big a subject to go into now; I would merely take the alpha and the omega. As to the alpha, we see Drake's partiality for "a middle-sized" ship. You will remember he chose for his flag-ship the 500 ton "Revenge," and a number of those ships appeared in the programme which followed the Armada. The omega, of course, is Nelson's fondness for seventy-fours.

So much for the argument on the general case. Now I have the rather less pleasant task of coming to the second part of my subject, which entails pointing out defective arguments and false or partial arguments. I quote again from a distinguished advocate of moderate speed: "A good position is more important than superior speed, and can be used to counterbalance the strategical advantages belonging to the latter." That is one of the arguments that appear in one form or other over and over again, that securing a good position is more important than superior speed. I cannot help feeling that that is very like saying that speed does not matter if you are only quick enough. It involves almost a logical absurdity—I do not use the word opprobriously, I mean a *reductio ad absurdum*—and it comes from neglecting the ascertained rules of strategical discussion.

It departs from those rules because it introduces personal and accidental factors. Really, such an argument is of no weight at all unless we are to assume that we always have available better positions than those of our enemy, or that we have greater strategical ability. Such assumptions are destructive of all scientific strategy. Most of the great writers have always laid it down that you must determine the normal first, and to do that you must eliminate all accidental and personal factors. First determine the normal, and when you have done that you can make any allowance you like for accidental and personal circumstances. Therefore, I would put it to you that the whole of that line of argument is contrary to the ascertained rules of discussion, and ought to be eliminated.

What it really comes to is, that it is an argument for tactical and strategical study, being quite as important as powerful arms in warfare. That is, I think, a proposition which nobody denies nowadays.

The second class of argument, if you can call it an argument, lies in the danger of contrasting speed with offensive and defensive fighting power. Of course, speed is as much a part of a fighting ship as a horse is of cavalry. It has no strategical or tactical significance except as part of a ship's offensive and defensive power. Therefore, stating the case in that way rather tends to beg the question, and should be avoided. It is not really very important, but the whole question is so difficult that it is just as well to be precise in statement in order to reduce the possibility of error. The real question, of course, is whether high speed or moderate speed gives the higher fighting power all round.

Then there is the fallacy of that dictum which is constantly repeated that a fleet is no faster than its slowest ship. Very often, speaking strategically, the converse is really the case. The whole principle of the "attack in general chase" rests on the truth that the speed of the chasing fleet is the speed of its fastest vessel, and that the speed of the chased fleet is the speed of its slowest ship. Therefore, one has to be very careful in founding any argument on a dictum of that kind. The case that is quoted in support of this argument is generally the battle of Quiberon, and that is quoted also as a case where tactics were more important than speed. I cannot quite understand that. So far as I can read about what happened at Quiberon, there were no tactics at all. Hawke certainly made a signal under his new "Additional Instruction," for the leading ships to form line as they chased, but they were in such a hurry that they did not do it, and the action was never more than a general chase. There were no tactics. It was simply a question of time and speed. Had Hawke had only a little more speed there is no doubt that the French would have suffered much more severely, and not given us half the trouble they did afterwards.

Next, there are certain doubtful deductions from history I should like to deal with; and one is the assumption that the prevalence of the "seventy-four" type in relatively large proportion in our sailing fleets, was due to the necessity being felt for numbers of units rather than for the power of each unit. Now, that assumption is used in order to condemn the increasing size of ships which is assumed to come about in our effort to combine high speed with endurance. I submit that there is no proof whatever of that. It is a mere assumption. The preference for the "seventy-four" type clearly may have been chiefly due to a desire for speed. In the few places where I have been able to find any reasons for the selection, the reason is superior speed and ability to work to windward, which, of course, was equivalent to speed in those days.

I should like to quote one of the passages referred to. It is from the pen of Kempenfeldt, who was probably the most scientific of all our real fighting men. In 1782 he was writing to Lord Sandwich about a squadron he wanted to have in the Soundings to act defensively against the combined fleet of France and Spain, which was supposed to be coming into the Channel, and he says: "Such a squadron should be composed of two-decked ships only, so as to ensure its purpose. It must have the advantage of the enemy in sailing." That is clearly a case where "seventy-fours" and lesser ships were chosen because of their speed. In dealing with this question historically, we must never forget that in sailing days the sea-speed of battle-ships tended to be in inverse ratio to their size: the bigger the ship the slower it was. The reverse is the case now. In the old days they could not get speed without very great sacrifices of what is called fighting power. To-day, clearly, that is not true, if we admit increase of tonnage.

There is another class of argument, which I will put under the head of failure to recognise recent changes in strategical conditions. Of course, such things do change, not so much as in tactics, but strategy does change, and I venture to submit that torpedoes, wireless telegraphy, and submarines have produced changes of strategical conditions—not fundamental, perhaps, but very important, and the chief importance is that they practically destroy between them the whole of the old system of blockade. The old naval strategy in its final developments, at least, was based on close blockade, and that is now impossible. The general opinion is that open blockade will have to take its place. Now open blockade involves finding a secure interior position—a position that is out of torpedo danger, yet close enough to ensure contact with the enemy's fleet if he attempts to secure his object or to interfere with yours. For example, the position which Admiral Togo took at Mesampho. If you think of it, the possibility of finding such interior positions depends entirely upon your speed and not at all upon your radius of action. A position which would be exterior by distance may become interior if you have superior speed. You will find that the size of the area within which open blockading positions may be sought, will be proportional to your speed. Captain Mahan sought to get over this argument for speed by showing that Admiral Togo could have intercepted the Russian fleet, even if it had been faster than his own. But his argument is only another instance of the error of the single case. All it really shows is, that the geographical accidents of the Japanese Sea were peculiarly favourable to the Japanese. It cannot possibly show anything else. To meet this argument we have only to refer to another case, which he has made peculiarly his own. It is he who, above all other people, taught us the real weakness of our Plymouth and Torbay positions, and demonstrated that they were not really interior positions with regard to Brest. But with anything like superior speed there would have been little difficulty about controlling Brest from either of them.

There is one more point. It is really the most difficult and the most important of all, and that is, that these distinguished officers and other writers, in arguing against high speed, have entirely omitted to consider defensive warfare. One can hardly blame them, because this omission is undoubtedly the characteristic disease of contemporary strategy. In times past a general defensive has been forced upon us, and it may be again. But that is not so much the question as this: that we must always use the defensive whatever we are doing.

We cannot possibly concentrate a fleet for great offensive movements without containing operations elsewhere. If outside the main offensive sphere, you have forces capable of taking the offensive by their numbers, so far, theoretically, is your strategy bad, because you have not concentrated as much as you might have concentrated at the vital point. You cannot get perfect concentration on any one point of the war, the secret of all strategy, without defensive operations elsewhere. Therefore, when we read in these arguments such expressions as, "The tradition of the British Navy is always to take the offensive," let us be on our guard. That expression is always used as though it excluded the defensive, whereas the foundation of all strategy is that the offensive connotes the defensive always. The worst of all mis-readings of British naval history is that extraordinary fetish of the offensive, as if the offensive were a thing that could stand by itself. It is a fetish that kills strategy. It grew up in the days when we had that easy command after Trafalgar. It killed strategy just as Trafalgar killed tactics. It was not the view of the great 18th century admirals. You have only to think of the meaning of that technical expression which so often recurs: "A fleet to attend the motions of the enemy." That was the defensive fleet, which was the foundation of all the work of our great strategists.

If you will bear with me a moment, I should like to quote a strong example of that. Let us take one again from Kempenfeldt, in 1779: "Much, I may say, all depends upon this fleet"—that was the fleet which was holding the mouth of the Channel against the allied fleet which was coming up to take command of our narrow seas. "Much, I may say, all depends upon this fleet; it is an inferior against a superior fleet. Therefore, the greatest skill and address is required to counteract the designs of the enemy, to watch and seize the favourable opportunities for action, to catch the advantage of making an effort at some or other feeble part of the enemy's line; or, if such opportunities do not occur, to hover near the enemy, keep him at bay, and prevent him attempting anything, but at risk or hazard, to command their attention and oblige them to think of nothing but being on their guard against your attack." That was Kempenfeldt's view of a defensive fleet, the fleet to attend the motions of the enemy. There are similar remarks of Nelson's, but never so clear as Kempenfeldt's. Here is another of his sayings, part of which I have already read to you: "When inferior to the enemy, and you have only a squadron of observation to watch and attend their motions, such a squadron should be composed of two-decked ships only, so as to ensure its purpose. It must have the advantage of the enemy in sailing, else, under certain circumstances, it will be liable to be forced to battle and give up some of its heavy sailers. It is highly necessary to have such a fighting squadron to hang on the enemy's fleet, as it will prevent their dividing into squadrons for intercepting your trade or spreading their ships for a more extensive view."* There are several others I could quote to you to the same effect. You will recollect that at that time we were making our great effort in the West Indies to prevent the French getting hold of them. We sent out every ship we could possibly spare from the home squadrons, and they were reduced to their lowest defensive level. Kempenfeldt was employed in the Channel, once as flag-captain and the second time as a junior flag officer. In all his letters and memoranda he points out that the way to work a defensive fleet is to avoid action, except on your own terms, to worry your enemy, and so on. But throughout all these utterances you find the whole thing is hanging on speed, speed, speed, the whole way through, as being the only possible manner in which the work can be done. In the opinion of those men undoubtedly a successful defensive depended on superior speed.

The truth seems to be that we cannot possibly maintain the defensive ourselves, or break the defensive, if the enemy adopts it against us, without superior speed. I need not remind you of those long, uninteresting years, which consume so much of our naval history, when France assumed the defensive. We could not break it, and she kept those old wars going year after year, simply because we were never able to force a decisive action when we had the chance. Speed is at least one way to get out of that difficulty. We cannot rely on our tactics being always superior. Although public writers abroad seem taken with the idea of the offensive, introduced by a somewhat loose reading of Captain Mahan's works, there are pretty clear signs that the Admiralty staffs are not. They know the power of the defensive when it is used as Kempenfeldt meant it to be used, and nothing but speed can give us any sure hope of breaking through that attitude.

---

*For these quotations from Kempenfeldt I am indebted to the kindness of Professor J. K. Laughten. They occur amongst Lord Barham's Papers which he is editing for the Navy Record Society.

ADMIRAL SIR N. BOWDEN SMITH, K.C.B.: I think that the Institution and the Service generally is much indebted to Mr. Julian Corbett for having brought this important question before us. You must be all aware from what you read in the daily press and periodicals that there is a great difference of opinion on this subject. On the one hand, we have two of the most distinguished writers amongst our flag officers who tell us that there is no great strategical or tactical value in speed, and their opinion seems to be shared by the well known writer, Captain Mahan, of the United States Navy. On the other side there are several officers who affirm that speed is of great importance, and there is an excellent paper by Lieut.-Commander Sims of the United States Navy, which puts the subject clearly before us, and is well worth studying. I think one of the greatest objections to high speed and consequently very large ships is a matter that has been touched upon by the lecturer, namely, possibility of loss by mine or torpedo. In that respect a large and valuable ship is as likely, or even more likely, to be destroyed by a mine than a smaller ship, and that is, to my mind, one of the great objections. The author alludes to "Barfleur," who states that high speed necessarily reduces the radius of action. That is so but I would rather have the speed and sacrifice to a certain extent the coal endurance, because you cannot increase the speed of a ship after she is once built, whereas you can to a certain extent supplement her coal endurance by taking with the fleet on long voyages or ocean cruises, vessels carrying coal or liquid fuel. This arrangement must be carried out in future warfare by all ships or squadrons carrying out operations far from their base, each ship taking every opportunity of replenishing her stock of fuel whenever possible. With regard to the value of speed, I would point out to those who say that it is of no great tactical or strategical value, that both by land and sea one great object in warfare has been that of getting to a certain place in a certain time. If you do not arrive at a rendezvous in the required time, the object for which you wanted to be in that position may be lost. Barfleur refers much to former history in support of his arguments against the value of high speed. Although I greatly appreciate his excellent writing, I do not agree with him in that respect, and I would like, if you would allow me, to make a few observations on the late battle in the Sea of Japan, with regard to which I have made some extracts from the writings of men who actually witnessed the action, or who were able to report it on very good authority, I understood the lecturer to say that a good position is better than superior speed.

MR. JULIAN CORBETT: That is from Barfleur.

ADMIRAL BOWDEN SMITH: Well, in the late battle off Tsu-shima it certainly was, I think, superior speed that enabled Togo to gain his great initial advantage. I do not think anybody can deny that superior speed must give choice of position before engaging. We know that the Japanese during the whole course of the action kept up a 15-knot speed, whereas the Russian ships generally were not able to steam more than 12 knots. One writer says that "this superiority of speed was not long in asserting its influence." Another account says that the Japanese in single line ahead were steaming at 15 knots, and were able thus to draw ahead and concentrate their fire on the leading Russian vessels. In fact, the Japanese superior speed gave Togo the coveted lead. The Russian Admiral Enquist and others repeatedly referred to the superior speed of the Japanese as conducing to their success. Perhaps we should not think too much of that statement because the defeated side naturally seek an excuse for being defeated, and they would take advantage of anything that seemed to show a cause for their great catastrophe. During the action the weather appears to have been very misty and the hostile fleet obscured from each other; in fact, they lost each other to a certain extent, the fleets becoming separated, although the battle was decided almost in the first hour. It was on the second day that Togo, who had not fully realized the havoc he had wrought amongst the Russian ships, succeeded in coming up with the remainder of their fleet and, surrounding those which were still in fighting condition, forced them to surrender. Had the Russians the speed of the Japanese ships some of them would certainly have escaped to

Vladivostock. As it was, out of 38 Russian vessels which commenced the action, we know that 22 were sunk, seven captured, seven disarmed and interned, and only two got away altogether free; whereas during the two days' fighting the Japanese only appear to have lost two destroyers and one torpedo-boat. I do not mean to say for a moment that it was the superior speed alone which mainly gave the Japanese their victory. They were doubtless far better seamen; they manoeuvred their ships much better, and their men were much better gunners. The Russian ships in their over-loaded state were too easily sunk or too readily turned turtle. Although the Japanese fire was so much more effective than that of the Russians, it must not be inferred that the Japanese ships were more heavily armed, because such was not the case; they were much more lightly gunned than the Russian fleet. The Russians had 26 12-inch guns against only 1G of the Japanese, and 15 10-inch guns against one of the Japanese, while of the smaller calibre guns the Japanese had the preponderance, carrying 30 guns of about 8-inch against 12 in the Russian ships. To show how ineffective the Russian fire was, the Japanese, as I have before stated, only lost three torpedo vessels and had only 116 killed and 538 wounded. On the Russian side they had the great loss in ships already mentioned, and we know that something like 6,000 prisoners were captured. As for the Russian dead and drowned, we shall probably never know the number. It is generally supposed that the Russians showed insufficient courage, whereas we know that some of their ships fought in the most gallant way and continued in action even when they were badly on fire, or in a sinking condition. I have ventured to make these remarks on this battle because Barfleur and other writers quote so much from past history and do not go sufficiently into the history of our own time. Although I realize the great cost of high speed, it appears to me to be a modern necessity. Of course, there must be a limit to speed, and you must not sacrifice everything to it. I was never able to understand why a few years ago we built eight scouts at a cost of about 2¼ millions entirely for speed and nothing else. In these days of wireless telegraphy news can be easily communicated, and in heavy weather a cruiser could carry out scouting duties when these scouts could not face the sea. The same remarks apply to some of the scouts now building. When it comes to fighting ships we must have a certain amount of speed, even in our battle-ships. All mail and passenger ships are increasing their speed, and in the Navy we must keep pace with the times.

VICE-ADMIRAL W. H. HENDERSON: When the question of speed was first brought forward by "Barfleur" I welcomed a scientific discussion on the subject, because I felt that we in the Service had not really realised its importance, that we had had no guiding lights to direct us on its scientific aspects. I need not say that I have been waiting and hoping for a rejoinder to those articles, and I beg to thank Mr. Julian Corbett for coming forward in the way he has done for the benefit of us all, and to state that I most thoroughly agree with what he has said in his paper.

THE CHAIRMAN (ADMIRAL THE HON. SIR E. R. FREMANTLE): I must ask your indulgence to allow me to say a few words before I go away, as I have to catch a train. We have heard a very instructive lecture from the philosophical and historical point of view, and it is not easy for us to criticise it or speak about it at short notice. There are, however, some points which we can take up and consider, but more requires further consideration, and I think that perhaps accounts for the reluctance of so many of the naval officers I see here to-day to come forward and enter upon any criticism on a subject of such great importance, and one that demands such close attention and close argument. But I will endeavour to make a few remarks, strictly confining myself to the question before us, namely, the value of speed. I have been for a long time an advocate of speed. I had the honour of reading a lecture to this Institution a good many years ago, entitled, "Speed as a Factor in Naval Warfare," and I treated the matter then principally from the strategical point of view. I do not propose to deal now, at all events at any length, with the strategical value of speed. As the lecturer says, the strategical value of speed is beyond doubt. I entirely agree with him that it is rather begging the question to say that if you have got the best admirals, if you have got the best position, if you have got the inner lines, then, to a great extent, you can dispense with speed. I venture to think that is not a fair line of argument, because if we are to argue the question at all from the philosophical point of view we must say that the admirals are the same and the strategical positions are the same. Strategy undoubtedly has been altered, and must be altered, to a limited extent by the weapons in use. Tactics must have some effect on strategy. But what has a much greater effect is undoubtedly the position which you are holding or wish to hold, in short, the theatre of operations. But beyond that I think there can be no doubt that strategy is eternal; the rules we have to follow are much the same as those that our ancestors had to follow. With that I will leave the question of strategy. Now, one point which the lecturer had dealt with is whether radius of action falls in proportion to rise of extreme speeds. It may be so theoretically: probably it is so. Of course, if you take a scout and fill her up with machinery she has very little room for coal, and she expends a great deal of coal, but that is an extreme case. But assuming you have one of the "County" class, of 23 knots, and another vessel which is capable of going no more than 20 knots, and you want to make a passage at the rate of 15 knots, you will find the 20-knot vessel is going pretty nearly at her top speed in a passage, say, to the West Indies, whereas the 23-knot vessel is going at comparatively easy speed, and you will probably find the 23-knot vessel is the more economical vessel, and has a larger radius of action at that speed than the vessel which was supposed to have the larger radius of action at that speed. I do not consider at all that it is correct to say that the radius of action falls in proportion with the rise of speed. Under the instances to which I have referred the argument is in favour of speed. We have had an appeal to history generally, and I think it is quite right that we should appeal to history. I am afraid nowadays there is too much assumption that all history is what is commonly called "ancient history," and that under these circumstances we can discard it. I do not think the lecturer thinks that, but to some extent he would almost appear to adopt that view in talking about Sir Thomas Hardy and scrapping ships. It is a question of a sense of proportion—what you ought to scrap. There is no doubt that "donkey" frigates and the small brigs were many of them dangerous. The "donkeys" certainly earned their name; they could neither fight nor run away. Many of the brigs went by the expressive names of coffins. Undoubtedly Sir Thomas Hardy, who was a sailor and one of the best First Sea Lords we ever had, was right that bigger ships were wanted and that to some extent it would be right to scrap the coffins and "donkey" frigates. To what extent that was carried I do not know, but if I recollect Sir Thomas Briggs, it was simply due to the fact that he did not like those inferior class of ships. He also advocated three-deckers. I recollect in very early days, when I first joined the Navy, Charley Napier used to write in *The Times* frequently urging the building of three-deckers as the things that were most necessary. I think for close action in those days three-deckers were the things that were necessary. There are several things said in the paper that are admirable. The tradition of the Service, the author says, since Elizabethan days has been towards getting the utmost possible speed, and a great sacrifice of fighting strength has been made for it. I daresay some of you will recollect Nelson's dictum with regard to three-deckers. He was not altogether against three-deckers. At Trafalgar, you will recollect, the first three ships of the weather line were all three-deckers, but, nevertheless, he said that two seventy-fours alongside were better than a three-decker a long way off. Appeal has been made to the French, and I think it is quite right that we should refer to the French on many of these points, because there is no doubt they are very thoughtful observers, that they study the matter in a more scientific manner than we do, and when they talk of the difference between ocean strategy and strategy in the narrow seas, there is a good deal to be said for their views. I think we can take some exception to the statement, made by the lecturer that the main function of the British fleet is to control narrow seas. It is certainly a very important function, but the main function of the fleet, I think, to quote Jurien de la Graviere, is to occupy the great ocean highways. I venture to think, in the position in which this country is now, our business is to occupy the great highways. It is most important to the stability of the Empire, and almost as important to the defence of this country. I think, personally, we have neglected too much the necessities which this Empire requires. When the lecturer talks, as he very properly does, of the bases which we have, he might more correctly have spoken of the bases which we had, because we have dropped a great many of them. I will conclude by just referring to what Captain Davelny writes in "*La lutte pour tempire de la Mer,*" published last year. He gives an interesting study of the battle off Tsushima, and he has studied the question tactically and strategically. "En definitive, la vitesse est bien un element tactique; il serait dangereux d'en conclure qu'elle est un arme." I think that is a very good definition. As the lecturer said, it is not an arm. The horse was not intended to fight, although he might trample down someone; he answers in the same way that speed may render a ship capable of ramming another. At the same time, it is not so much an arm as it is an element in the fleet. Politvosky is the name of the gentleman who wrote to his wife, and whose letter was published after his death at Tsu-shima. He was in the Russian Navy, the Chief Constructor, as we should call him. He gives pretty fully the damage which took place in Rodjestvensky's fleet, and tells us how extremely slow it was. I think it was the Russian Captain Semenoff who mentioned the difference of speed between the two fleets as something like six knots. We do not know what the difference of speed was, but it was probably very great. From Politvosky's account and from the speed which Rodjestvensky's fleet kept in their passage from Tangiers to Madagascar, I think they averaged 117 miles a day—very little more than sailing speed, chiefly due to the new ships, which were constantly breaking down. While on that I should like to say one word with regard to what the lecturer said about the fast fleet and the slow fleet. I have a note here with regard to the fallacy of the dictum that a fleet is no faster than its slowest ship, where the author says "As often as not the converse is nearer the truth," and that the decisive speed of the chasing fleet is that of its fastest ships. I do not think it is a fallacy speaking generally. I think it is accurate. He defined it accurately in his speech, but not in his summary. I was going to say that it was generally true, but more so for the chased than the chasing fleet. The chased fleet speed is as the slowest ship, and it is true to say that chasing speed is that of the fastest ship. There is one more summing up of Captain Davelny that I should like to mention. He says, "La vitesse est l'auxiliare de la force; elle ne peut la remplacer. Il ne faut s'en servir qu'avec discernement, et il semble bien que Togo n'aurait pas deux fois, perdu de vue l'enemi s'il avait marcho moins vite." In fact it is perfectly clear that twice Togo did lose the Russian fleet, but each time he was able to come up with it and bring on the action again. The same thing almost happened on the 10th of August. Twice he got behind and both times he was able to pick up the Russian fleet again. If that is not of value, whether you call it strategical or tactical, I do not know what is of value. I have mentioned the question of scrapping. What the lecturer says seems to me, in his opinion, practically to justify the amount of scrapping we have had in the Navy, but for my part I cannot agree with it. There is a tendency to scrap still further, and I think it is an extremely dangerous tendency. However, we are not talking politics here now, and I will not dwell upon that. I do not think the lecturer said enough about the fact that if we are to have very high speed, and also all the offensive and defensive power that is now necessary on the first-class battle-ship, the question of size will have to be taken into consideration. The size keeps constantly increasing. I think on that subject Mahan is on sound ground, as is also the writer on naval policy, Barfleur. One does not see where it is to end. It is a truism that has been repeated over and over again, but is always being forgotten, that however big the ship is she is in danger of being blown up by a sub-marine mine. The bigger the ship the fewer the units we can have, and consequently the more difficult it is to detach a couple of battle-ships or anything of that sort. Under these circumstances there is room for a good deal of argument with regard to the extreme size to which we are going. It is not a point on which one can be dogmatic at all. It may be absolutely right to build "Dreadnoughts," and I do not say it is not. I am not prepared to say anything. If it *is* right to have a single armament of very heavy guns, as we have in the "Dreadnought"—and it is more a question of gunnery than anything else—I think it is necessary to have "Dreadnoughts." But we want ships for a good many purposes in warfare, not only scouting, protection of commerce, getting information, landing at some place or other, lending a little assistance to some person or other, but for twenty different circumstances. There is the history of the wars of the Mediterranean in 1797–8, our wars with France afterwards, the actions of Lord Cochrane on the coasts of France and Spain, of Nelson on the coast of Italy or at Corsica, when he had to embark soldiers, and all that sort of thing. None of these are scouting or protection of commerce, and yet they are the everyday use to which you have to put ships in a war. Under those circumstances we do want numbers, and that is an argument not sufficiently dwelt upon. I entirely agree with Barfleur, who says that if there was a war to-morrow want of cruisers would be found written in the hearts of many admirals. We appeal to history, and it shows that the number of small vessels increased largely after we had absolute command of the seas following Trafalgar. I thank you for having listened to me, and I am very sorry to have to go away. I should like to have heard the rest of the discussion. Before I leave I wish to express my thanks to Mr. Julian Corbett for having come here to-day. I feel that the lecture is one of the greatest value, and I feel it was a great compliment to ask me to come and preside. I am only sorry I cannot do more justice to the situation, as it is a subject which interests me very much.

MR. JULIAN CORBETT, IN REPLY, SAID:—I should like to express my great satisfaction at having received such high endorsement as has been my good fortune this afternoon. With regard to some of the omitted arguments, I know that I have omitted nearly all the arguments that tell against high speed, but that is simply because they have been so admirably put by more capable people already. My real reason for coming here was to put the other side of the case, as Admiral Henderson was kind enough to say. An impression seemed to be abroad that there was very little to be said on the other side, and that was due to the extreme ability of the officers who had ventured to doubt whether, in the matter of speed, we are not going too far. As I said, that seems to me a most desirable thing to have done, but I could not help feeling that in the enthusiasm of trying to shake our too self-confident position on the question of speed, they had been carried a little further than they wanted to go when they started, and that the time had come when one ought to put forward the general grounds on which the old tradition in favour of speed seemed to rest. With regard to concentration on the van, it was a point I omitted. It is constantly said that the power which superior speed gives you of concentrating on the enemy's van can be easily neutralised by his turning away. I submit that it is not a sufficient argument, because it admits the fact that superior speed tactically gives you the power of controlling your enemy's course. It is surely a great strategical advantage to be able even to turn your enemy off the course he is trying to take. I am sure cases will suggest themselves to your imagination where such a tactical advantage might decide a whole campaign by preventing the enemy continuing the course which it was necessary for him to continue in order to attain his object. Therefore, when you say that superior speed can be neutralised tactically by the power of turning away, although you are denying the tactical advantage of speed, you are giving it an enormous strategical importance. With regard to Sir Edmund Fremantle's remark, that I seemed to wish to wipe out the whole of history, as that happens to be my profession, it is not very likely that is what I meant. What I did mean was, that just as I am too much inclined, perhaps, to give weight to old examples, so officers are inclined to give too much weight to recent examples. For tactics, perhaps, that is not a very objectionable course. But when you are dealing with strategy it is extremely dangerous to deal with a few recent examples, because although they may cover the tactical ground, they cannot possibly cover the whole of the strategical ground. Therefore, what I meant was precisely the opposite, that for strategy the old examples are really of more value than the modern ones, simply because they are more numerous.

CHAPTER THREE

The Role of Maritime International Law in Grand Strategy

C orbett's thinking on maritime belligerent rights was already clear in 1896, when he stressed that the power to blockade and capture outlying territory gave "England, in spite of her military weakness, so commanding a position in Europe." He also examined the legal basis of enforcement.[1] He returned to the subject in 1907 with "The Capture of Private Property at Sea," his second Fisher-inspired essay in *The Nineteenth Century and After*, which provided intellectual rigor to the Admiralty's attempt to prevent the Liberal government from agreeing to any further limitation on maritime belligerent rights at the Second Hague Convention.[2]

Corbett attacked the position adopted by the Lord Chancellor, Robert Threshie Reid, First Baron Loreburn, a lawyer who served as a Cabinet minister and head of the British legal system. He argued that Loreburn's call for the abolition of maritime belligerent rights, especially that of blockade and the capture of enemy property on neutral merchant ships, at sea, would serve the interests of continental military powers, which had always sought to restrict the impact of sea power on land. Corbett derided the British concession of "Free Ships—Free Goods" that allowed enemy property to travel safely on neutral ships, calling it a serious self-inflicted injury that had weakened national strategy. He separated the immunity of private property from that of neutral or free ships, making enemy goods on board free from capture, citing International Law to demonstrate that the right to take or destroy enemy property was a universally accepted, legitimate means of coercing the enemy. Corbett made the case that any restraints adopted on land were for operational convenience, to maintain troop discipline or avoid guerrilla action, and did not prevent the occupation from coercing the enemy to submit, citing German practice in the Franco-Prussian War of 1870–1871. He also attacked Loreburn's confused attitudes toward contraband and local blockades as indistinguishable morally from general blockades and advised him to read the correspondence of Philip Yorke, First Earl of Hardwicke, his eighteenth-century predecessor, in order to understand British policy and practice. Corbett also cited Mahan's *War of 1812* in support of the British position. Corbett dismissed the argument that land transport would render blockades ineffective despite the most prominent advocate of such views of Halford Mackinder, Corbett's personal friend. The right to capture was, Corbett stressed, the key to British security and deterrence—the only thing that made war at sea useful. Fisher's support enabled Mahan to reprint the paper in his 1907 essay collection *Some Neglected Aspects of War*.

Corbett based much of the legal argument of *Some Principles* on the logic he laid out in the 1907 paper, although he toned down the attack on Loreburn. In his 1911 book, *Some Principles of Maritime Strategy*, Corbett focused on establishing correct principles, demolishing the fallacies that littered the field. These ranged from extreme "blue-water" arguments, which reckoned battle victory would win a war, to the Liberal "Free Seas" dogma that wanted to allow the enemy to trade in wartime. In this book Corbett demonstrated that economic warfare was the primary instrument of maritime strategy against continental states. It was the reason why Britain, perhaps alone, had the capacity to make truly limited war. The purpose of securing command of the sea was to allow a dominant navy "to exert direct military pressure upon the national life of our enemy ashore." The stoppage of commerce was the maritime equivalent of the conquest of territory. Corbett also took the trouble to invest this strategy with a moral quality: "commerce prevention" caused less human suffering than any other form of war, being closer to a legal action than a military operation. He also laid the foundations for the "distant" economic warfare methods of the First World War. "Admit of the principle of tactical or close blockade, and as between belligerents you cannot condemn the principle of strategical or distant blockade. Except in their effect upon neutrals, there is no juridical difference between the two."

The exception was revealing: the "neutrals" he had in mind were the Americans. The United States would hamper the implementation of British economic warfare in the First World War, but only until it joined the war in April 1917. As soon as the fighting stopped, American opposition to British principles resumed.

Wars, Corbett stressed, were ended by the ability of one side to "exert pressure on the citizens and their collective life," citing German General Colmar von der Golz, who wrote of "forcing a peace" by making "the enemy's country feel the burdens of war with such weight that the desire for peace will prevail." Without the right to capture private property there would be little purpose to naval activity, beyond defense against invasion; blockade pressure could only be applied through such barbarous methods as indiscriminate coastal bombardment and raids. Indeed, the general tenor of war, if all similar rights were denied, would be reduced to a "purely legal procedure." Not only was the world unready for such a change, but the effect would be to deprive those seeking to preserve the peace, who Corbett expected to be the British, of their greatest deterrent.

Corbett argued that economic warfare, including the capture of enemy property, was Britain's basic strategic weapon.

To limit it without applying equal constraint to operations of land would be unrealistic, while any significant change in the legal rights of belligerents on either land or sea element would make war more and not less likely. He supported his views with historical evidence and legal reasoning. Later his target would become the as-yet-unratified 1911 Declaration of London and those in Britain who supported it; among them, Loreburn was the most significant.[3]

The other major target for Corbett's work on international law was the Army, which was advocating with some success the need to join the French army in Europe as an alternative to the normal British strategy of limited maritime war. Corbett's arguments helped prevent any move by the Cabinet to adopt a continental strategy, leaving the question of national policy open until war broke out in 1914. Fisher distributed the essay widely, to Cabinet ministers, the king, British journalists, and even the American delegate at The Hague. More than any other public contribution, the essay helped to secure the strategic impact of sea power.

By actively shaping the legal framework, nations can shift the strategic balance between land and sea or air: this was Corbett's main theme. He wanted Britain to shape a legal system that enhanced sea power against land power, because Britain was never going to be a continental state. As a lawyer he recognized that limiting economic warfare would oblige Britain to mobilize more soldiers, and as a strategist he recognized this would be a false move.

Shaping the legal context of war has never mattered more. Few modern servicemen will escape obligations imposed by internationally agreed legal texts like the United Nations Convention of the Law of the Sea, even if their own government might not actually be a signatory. Such was the position Britain faced in 1914—it had not ratified the latest agreements but felt obliged to apply them anyway to avoid problems with potentially dangerous neutrals—in this case the United States of America.

THE CAPTURE OF PRIVATE PROPERTY AT SEA

June 1907

"As things stand at present," writes Professor Perels in the last edition of his *Internationale Seerecht*, "we cannot count on the exemption of private property at sea from capture in the near future. The main factor is that the British Government since the Declaration of Paris has maintained an attitude of persistent and determined resistance to all movements for reforming the laws of maritime warfare." Publicists of almost all countries, including our own, have been expressing themselves in similar terms, and we are warned by some of our best international lawyers that there is growing up abroad a mass of hostile opinion on the subject which it is unsafe for us to ignore. Professor Perels' words conveniently focus for us that alleged mass of opinion, and since he was formerly Admiralitatsrath and is now Departements Direktor in Reichs-Marine Amt and Professor in the Berlin University, we may take his formula as something like our official arraignment at the bar of Europe. But before examining the charge with a view to preparing a defence it is wise at once to enter a claim to vary the indictment. We do not deny the "persistent and determined resistance." We merely beg to submit that our "persistent and determined resistance" has been "to all movements for reforming the laws of maritime warfare *in the interests of the great military States.*"

It is true that some of our most respected authorities would persuade us that the exemption of private property at sea from capture is particularly to our own interests, because we possess the largest, and therefore, as they assume, the most vulnerable mercantile marine, and because we rely for our sustenance more than any other nation on seaborne supplies.

Julian Corbett, "The Capture of Private Property at Sea," *The Nineteenth Century and After,* June 1907. Reprinted in A. T. Mahan, *Some Neglected Aspects of War* (Boston: 1907); Donald M. Schurman, *Julian S. Corbett, 1854–1922: Historian of British Maritime Policy from Drake to Jellicoe* (London: Royal Historical Society, 1981).

But this is a military question, on which our publicists are not safe guides. It involves strategical considerations, which clearly they have not taken into account, and their view is not shared by the Navy. It is a view, however, which is seriously urged by serious people, and we must return to it. For the present it is enough to claim that the leading facts in the history of the movement create a *prima facie* case that exemption is for the benefit of weak fleets and powerful armies. Started originally by a French abbé, the idea was first embodied in a treaty by Frederick the Great, a man who had had practical experience of how gravely the vulnerability of commerce at sea may affect the progress of a Continental war. When he was in alliance with Great Britain it did not occur to him to make the suggestion. It was the newborn Republic of America that proposed it to him; and he wisely agreed, since the arrangement made it impossible for the United States ever to make war on him at all. Similarly, the United States was wise to get the sanction of so great a figure to the principle of immunity, since her budding commerce was always at the mercy of her one enemy so long as capture was permitted. With material advantages so great and obvious in hand it can convince nobody to talk of lofty and disinterested ideals.

Next it was Napoleon who put forward the new doctrine, and sought to establish it by the revolutionary violence of his "Continental System." In 1866, Austria, cooped up in the head of the Adriatic by the menace of a superior Italian fleet, declared for it. Italy, similarly threatened by France, had already done so. Again, in 1870 Prussia magnanimously intimated that, true to the sublime principles of Frederick the Great, it was her intention, whatever France did, to treat as sacred all innocent private property at sea.

When the buffalo found the lion in his path, he exclaimed, with a superb gesture, "For my part, I mean to remain true to my vegetarian principles."

Now to examine the charge more seriously and with what temper we can. For it must be understood that our friends abroad make their accusation opprobriously. We are represented as standing in the way of human progress, of obstructing for our own selfish ends the march of civilization, of seeking to perpetuate the methods of barbarism, of thwarting the disinterested aspirations of nobler nations to mitigate the severity of war and humanize its practice. And all this because, as they say, we refuse to complete the work of the Declaration of Paris by consenting to give to private property at sea that complete sanctity which it is unblushingly alleged to enjoy in warfare on land. So shocking does such depravity sound that in many cases our serious and high-minded journalism, which is so dear to us, is beginning to ask, in its most moving and conscientious tones, if we are to be the last of all nations to recognize this sacred duty to humanity.

Were it not that this particular attitude towards the question was so ludicrous it would be difficult to treat it with patience. Such a charge against ourselves is peculiarly hard, seeing that we have to our credit a record in respect of the mitigation of war which no nation can pretend to rival. There is no nation that can point to such a concession to the public opinion of the world against interest as we made in consenting, in 1856, to the doctrine of "Free ships, free goods." At the time it was widely regarded, and is still so regarded, as depriving us of one of the most powerful weapons in our armory; and yet for the sake of goodwill amongst nations, for the sake of softening the hardships of war to neutrals, we surrendered that right. For centuries we had clung to it as essential to the maintenance of our sea power; yet a higher and more farsighted wisdom pressed for the almost quixotic sacrifice, and it was done. Can any nation show a sacrifice beside it? Let him who can cast the first stone at us now.

To add to the unreasonableness of our accusers, instead of acknowledging handsomely the lengths to which we went on that occasion, they rail at us because we will not extend the principle to the complete immunity of private property at sea. As though the one principle had anything to do with the other. "You might as well say," said Sir William Harcourt during a debate on the point in 1878—and surely he, whether as a Liberal humanitarian or an international lawyer, should carry weight enough—"You might as well say that the extension of the Great Western Railway would be an extension of the Great Northern. They do not go in the same direction, they have not the same object, they are not parallel in any respect." Nothing can serve better for clearing the subject of fallacies and exhibiting the true grounds of the British attitude than to follow out the line of reasoning which the great international jurist indicated in opposing the idea on that occasion.

If the ideas which determined the status of private property in war be traced back to the dawn of modern international law, we shall find Grotius, in 1625, and Bynkershoek a century later, giving as an axiom the right to confiscate or destroy all property whatsoever belonging to an enemy wherever found. The axiom was quickly modified by Vattel, who wrote during the Seven Years' War. While admitting the abstract right, he maintained that its exercise should only be permitted as far as it is called for by the purposes of war. Here we have the first application of the true theory of war to the question. We make war not for the purpose of doing the enemy all the harm we can, but to bring such pressure to bear upon him as will force him to do our will—that is, will convince him that to make peace on our terms is better than continuing to fight. Now, the indiscriminate plunder of private property and its wanton destruction, while causing an immense amount of individual suffering, do not contribute in the most forcible way to the kind of pressure that is needed. Consequently, it had already become the practice for an invading enemy to treat private property with a certain respect, or rather, perhaps, economy, and to endeavor to set some restraint upon its indiscriminate plunder and destruction.

It is to this movement is due the oft-repeated but wholly unfounded assertion that private property ashore, unlike private property at sea, has been made generally immune from capture. It is further asserted that this immunity was due to a growing sense of humanity and a Christian desire to mitigate the horrors of war. Now, this is the kind of assertion which makes plain and practical people impatient with international law and blinds them to its value and reality. It is just one of those expressions which jurists let slip from a mere habit of the pen. Of this particular statement, that the restrictions in question were due to a growing sense of humanity, there is no real evidence whatever. Humanity may have been a contributory cause, but, if we turn from the loose expressions of jurists to the dry light of the orders actually promulgated by invading generals, we see at once that the real reason of the restrictions was strategical and military, and not moral at all. Take, for instance, the earliest case as typical—the rule of Gustavus Adolphus against plundering: "If it is so please God that we beat the enemy either in the field or in his leaguer, then shall every man follow the chase of the enemies; and no man give himself up to fall upon the pillage so long as it is possible to follow the enemy," etc. This germ idea that pillage actually lessens your power to exert the necessary pressure was further developed by the rules of Frederick the Great; but he took a long step further. For that great master of war recognized not only that pillage demoralized and weakened the weapon with which the pressure had to be exerted, but that pillage and destruction were not the most profitable or effective ways of exercising your rights over the enemy's property. To deprive the enemy's people of their power to produce was both to destroy the value of your conquest and its power of maintaining your troops. To protect the goose and enable her to continue laying her golden eggs was the only sound policy. He therefore insisted on the method of war exercising his war right by levying contributions and making requisitions. By this means he at once maintained the temper of his weapon and made the pressure of the occupation more lasting, more powerful, and more directly coercive to the collective life of the enemy. To say that he abandoned his right over enemy's property is to play with words. "If an army is in winter quarters in an enemy's country," he writes in his *General Principles of War*, "the soldiers receive gratis bread, meat, and beer, which are furnished by the country." And again: "The enemy's country is bound to supply horses for the artillery, munitions of war, and provisions, and to make up any deficiencies of money." The truth is that no restraint of the old rule of Grotius and Bynkershoek is to be found that does not operate to the military or strategical benefit of the belligerent, not one that does not directly increase the pressure which the invading force is seeking to exert to achieve its end. The principle reached its clearest expression during the Franco-German war, where it was absolutely essential to German success that they should not goad the French people into guerilla warfare, as Napoleon had done in Spain, by permitting irresponsible exercise of belligerent rights over private property. By the German orders of 1870 no requisition could be made except by general officers or officers in command of detached corps.

The system worked admirably, and, on the whole, as mercifully and with as little individual suffering as is possible in war. The object of an invasion—the means by which it exerts the necessary pressure—is to produce a stagnation of national life. This the German invasion did effectively, and the stagnation grew deeper and more intolerable the more it was prolonged, till submission was recognized to be the lesser evil. But all this was not done merely by the victories of armies. It was done by the exercise of belligerent rights over enemy's property: of the right to seize and consume it; of the right to control roads and railways and inland waters, so as to prevent its flow and render commerce impossible except in so far as it suited the belligerent; and of the right to carry military execution against it in case of resistance by its owners. Without the right to requisitions and contributions, without the right to control civil communications, it could not be done. War, as is universally admitted, would become impossible. Nations cannot be brought to their knees by the mere conflict of armies, any more than they can by the single combats of kings. It is what follows victory that counts—the choking of the national life by process of execution on property, the stagnation produced by the stoppage of civil communications, whether public or private. Here is a picture of what the process meant, drawn by the able pen of a man who saw it face to face in 1870:

> In occupied towns officials receive no salaries, professional men no fees. The law courts are closed. Holders of house property can get no rent. Holders of land can neither get rent, nor can they cultivate the soil or sell their crops. The State funds pay no dividends, or, if they do, all communication between occupied and unoccupied districts being broken off, the dividends cannot be touched. Railway dividends are equally intangible, and perhaps the line on which the shareholder has especially counted is in the hands of the enemy.

This is what conquest of territory means—the prostration of the national life; and this is why conquest of territory is the means by which land warfare seeks to gain its end.

With this picture in our minds of the way in which private property is dealt with ashore, and the way in which it is made to contribute to the victor's object, let us turn to the sea, and inquire in what manner its treatment there is less moral, less human, or less necessary, if war is to be waged at all. To begin with, we note that in some respects private property has never been so badly treated at sea as it has been on land;

at least, in modern times and in regular warfare it has never been the subject of indiscriminate plunder. The ruthless scramble for loot, which led to the acutest suffering and cruelty ashore, was no part of sea capture. Prizes were taken by orderly act of war, were regularly condemned, and the proceeds divided amongst the captors in cool blood and by authority. Again, at sea immediate military execution was never the penalty for resisting interference with private property, as it always was, and in some cases still is, ashore. The real reason why capture at sea got a bad name was due to privateers, by whom the greater part of it was done, and who in some areas, and particularly in the Mediterranean, were often guilty of unspeakable horrors. The evil was early recognized by Great Britain, and during the Seven Years' War an Act was passed forbidding the granting of commissions to vessels under a certain tonnage, in order to ensure that the work should be done by respectable merchant captains, and not by mere smugglers and pirates. It is not, of course, pretended that this law was made from merely philanthropic reasons, any more than was our concession about "free ships, free goods." Though a sense of honor did enter into it, the chief reason was that we found ourselves unable to control the lawlessness of small privateers, and felt that neutrals, whom we did not wish to exasperate, had a legitimate cause of complaint. Now the abuse is no longer possible, since the Declaration of Paris abolished privateering. Over and above this great mitigation of the hardships of warfare against private property at sea, there must also be taken into consideration the spread of the practice of marine insurance, which now distributes the initial loss by individuals over the general capital of the nation. The result is that even the most convinced advocates of the change, both at home and abroad, admit that the argument from inhumanity is untenable. The Lord Chancellor, himself our strongest advocate of reform, has plainly declared that "no operation of war inflicts less suffering than the capture of unarmed vessels at sea."

The truth is that the sea service, in demanding the retention of its right to general capture, asks no more than what is universally granted to the land service. It asks no more than to exercise war rights over property in so far as, in the words of Vattel, it is called for by the purposes of war—in so far as the pressure necessary to bring peace cannot be exerted without it. It asks only to be allowed to produce that stagnation of the enemy's life at sea which an army is permitted to produce ashore by conquest of territory. And how can such stagnation be produced? Not by conquest, for conquest of the sea is impossible. The sea cannot be the subject of ownership. You cannot do more, however complete your ascendancy, than deprive your enemy of his use of the sea; you can do no more than deny him that part of his national life which moves and has its being on the sea. This is what we mean when we speak of "command of the sea," and not "conquest of the sea." The value of the sea internationally is as a means of communication between States and parts of States, and the use and enjoyment of these communications is the actual life of a nation at sea. The sea can be nothing else, except a fishing-ground, and fishing is comparatively so small a factor in war nowadays that it may be eliminated from the question. All, then, that we can possibly gain from our enemy upon the sea is to deny him its use and enjoyment as a means of communication. Command of the sea means nothing more nor less than control of communications. It occupies exactly the same place and discharges the same function in maritime warfare that conquest and occupation of territory does in land warfare. If one is lawful and necessary, so is the other; if both are lawful and necessary, then each connotes the legality and necessity of the means by which alone the condition of stagnation can be brought about.

At sea this condition is produced by dealing with private property on exactly the same principle as on land—that is to say, in the most economical and effective manner. By its capture and conversion to the use of the navy we make it contribute directly to the force and economy of our weapon, and by an orderly system of prize regulations we do it without in any way demoralizing our *personnel* or goading the enemy's people to irregular retaliation. By no other means can we do what ashore is done by contributions and requisitions—that is, by no other means can we make enemy's property serve to a merciful and speedy end to hostilities. By this means also we control the enemy's communications, we paralyze his seaborne commerce, we sever him from his outlying territory. By no other means can we mercifully and effectively deprive him of all the sea can give him, and produce the state of stagnation of his maritime life that conquest of territory does of his life ashore.

By the victories of fleets alone it can no more be done than by the victories of armies.

If, then, in this way we test the doctrine of immunity of private property in the cold light of the theory of war—if we keep in mind that war consists of two phases—firstly, the destruction of the enemy's armed forces, and, secondly, of pressure on the population to produce stagnation of national life, we see the answer to our great military neighbors is complete. When they ask us to abandon the right of capture of private property at sea—of dealing with it, that is, in the most merciful and effective way for achieving the purposes of war—we reply, We will do so when you abandon the right of requisition and contribution. And when they ask us, as in effect they do, to give up the right of controlling sea communications, we reply, We will do so when you give up the right to control roads, railways, and inland waters. If they go further—as they fairly may—and ask, "What about the hardship of detaining the crews of captured merchantmen?" we answer, "We will abandon that means of stopping your commerce also, when you abandon forced labor of the civil population ashore." It is all a *reductio ad absurdum*. Without the exercise of such rights both conquest of territory and command of the sea become nugatory and war impossible.

But our opponents may reply, We do not ask you to give up control of communications. We would leave you commercial blockade. But is this what they mean? It is true that many of them except commercial blockade from their claim, but what the Lord Chancellor demands is entire exemption of private property, "unless really contraband or its place of destination be a beleaguered fortress." This, of course, amounts to a complete prohibition of our right to control communications except for the purpose of destroying the enemy's armed forces. It prohibits it for the purpose of the secondary process of pressure, and is entirely inadmissible. The Chancellor's meaning is at least perfectly clear. What is difficult to believe is that those who express themselves less roundly can really mean anything else. Let us examine what the position of these men leads to. In effect they say, We admit your abstract right to capture private property at sea, but deny that its general capture on the high seas is necessary for the purposes of war. This point of view is so plausible that it has highly commended itself to our own advocates of immunity. Ignoring the whole theory of maritime warfare, that it is a mere question of controlling communications, they argue as though all we could gain from general capture on the high seas is the paltry value of the goods seized. It was just Lord Granville's attitude at the momentous meeting of the Secret Committee of the Council on the eve of the Seven Years' War, when, on the question of whether admirals at sea should be ordered to seize French merchantmen, he declared he was against "vexing your neighbors for a little muck." If we regard the mere value of the property captured, this is true enough. It represents no more than the captor's attempt to subsist his fleet on the sea he commands, as ashore an army is subsisted on the territory it conquers. But the attempt never leads to much. The best we can do at sea by a complete conversion of all we can lay hands on is but a trifle compared with what is gained ashore by the process of contribution, requisition and forced labor. It is, indeed, not a little hard that the military Powers should scold us for nibbling this sorry crust when they habitually gorge themselves on baskets of loaves.

But though intrinsically the capture of property on the high seas has an almost negligible military value, as a deterrent its value is beyond measure. For it is an essential part of the process of destroying the enemy's commerce by control of sea communication. Blockade alone—even if blockade in the old sense were still possible—will not do. In their best days blockades were never thoroughly effective. It is the feeling that a ship and her cargo are never safe from capture from port to port that is the real deterrent, which breaks the heart of merchants and kills their enterprise. But this is a point on which all may not agree. It matters little, for it is not the one that is fatal to our reformers' claim.

The fatal point is this—that if you admit the only form of blockade that is possible under present conditions, and refuse the right of general capture, you establish a law so unfairly advantageous to Great Britain that no other Power could possibly be expected to assent to it, and we ourselves would certainly not have the effrontery to propose it.

The current conception of effective blockade is that agreed upon between England and Russia in 1801: the port blockaded must be watched by ships anchored before it or stationed sufficiently near to make egress or ingress obviously dangerous. All countries have adopted this idea. But this was before the day of torpedoes. The idea was, as actually expressed in certain Dutch treaties, that the blockading ships should be as close in as was compatible with safety from the enemy's coast defence. The defence in those days was guns. But what now of mobile defence? Is a blockading fleet entitled to be so far out as to be beyond torpedo-boat or destroyer range? If so it must be completely out of sight, and egress and ingress cannot be manifestly dangerous, and the blockading squadron must be cruising far from the port and far from territorial waters. If such distant and invisible blockade is not to be recognized as effective, then effective blockade is now impossible, and no means of controlling sea communications remains except general capture. It follows, then, that if the Continental Powers admit our right to control communication and deny us general capture, they must recognize such distant blockade as effective and lawful.

Now let us see how the law would work. In the case of war with France (which, being the most unlikely one, may be taken with least offence), it would be admissible for us to station a squadron, say, off Yarmouth and stretch a chain of cruisers from the Lizard to Cape Ortegal, and declare a blockade of the whole of the French Atlantic and Channel ports. Then, after due notice, every neutral and every Frenchman leaving a French port or consigned to one that appeared on the scene would be liable to be captured and sent in for judgment for attempted breach of blockade. The same liability, moreover, by the law of ultimate destination, would attach to such ships *in transitu* in any part of the world. In the case of Russia or Germany a similar situation could be set up still more easily, assuming we had once obtained a working command of the sea. On the other hand, it would be practically impossible for all these three Powers combined to set up such a situation against us; unless, indeed, in the unimaginable eventuality of their being relatively strong enough to maintain a blockading chain from Finisterre through the Faroes to the coast of Norway. It is a pure question of geography. If, then, the doctrine of permitting blockade in its sole possible form and refusing general capture were adopted, we could always paralyze the ocean-borne commerce of any of the great military Powers, while they, being unable to blockade effectively, and not being allowed to make prizes on the high seas, could not possibly touch ours. It is not to be believed that your well-meaning advocates of justice between nations can really intend an arrangement so grossly unjust. Clearly there is but one alternative—either you must leave the law as it is, or adopt the candid proposal of the Chancellor and abolish capture of private property altogether, saving only contraband and military blockade. And what the Chancellor's proposal would mean must be kept clearly in mind. It would permit us to deal with private property for the purpose of overpowering the armed force of the enemy, and deny us the right to use it for reaping the fruit of success.

Turning now from the Continental Powers to America, we find that the best naval opinion there is entirely with us. The contention on which we rely is really this—that the right to capture merchantmen and their cargoes does not depend on the primitive right over enemy's property so much as on the right and necessity of controlling our enemy's communications. Let us see how it is treated by Captain Mahan, who, above all men, by his genius and learning is entitled to give judgment. His declaration is the more remarkable because America has always been the most prominent champion of immunity and the most ardently convinced that in advocating the reform she was upholding the cause of civilization, humanity, and justice. This belief with the mass of the people has survived her taking rank as a great naval Power, and must be treated with respect. For all their practical plain sense the Americans are idealists at heart, more so, perhaps, than any other people, and it therefore required no little courage and the deepest conviction for Captain Mahan to stand up and tell his countrymen their feeling of magnanimity was false, mistaken, and contrary to plain sense and justice. Yet so he does in his latest work *The War of 1812*, calmly, cogently, and without flinching. In that work he discloses a ripe study of the theory of war which none of his others contain in the same degree—and for the full development of that theory, be it remembered, we are indebted mainly to the Germans themselves—and here is the result of its application to the question before us:

> The claim for private property [he says] . . . involves a play upon words, to the confusion of ideas, which from that time [that is, from Napoleon's Continental System] to this has vitiated the arguments upon which have been based a prominent feature of American policy. Private property at a standstill . . . is the unproductive money in a stocking hid in a closet.

Property belonging to private individuals, but embarked in the process of transportation and exchange, which we call commerce, is like money in circulation. It is the life-blood of national prosperity, on which war depends, and as such is national in its employment, and only in owner-ship private. To stop such circulation is to sap national prosperity, and to sap prosperity, on which war depends for its energy, is a measure as truly military as is killing of the men whose arms maintain war in the field. Prohibition of commerce is enforced at will when an enemy's army holds a territory. If permitted it inures to the benefit of the conqueror. . . . It will not be doubted that, should a prohibition on shore be disregarded, the offending property would be seized as punishment. . . . The seizure of enemy's merchant ships and goods for violating the prohibition against their engaging in commerce is what is commonly called the seizure of private property. Under the methods of the last two centuries it has been in administration a process as regular legally as is libelling a ship for an action in damages; nor does it differ from it in principle. The point at issue is not "Is the property private?" but "Is the method conductive to the purposes of war?" Property strictly private on board ship, but not in process of circulation, is for this reason never touched, and to do so is considered as disgraceful as a common theft.

He then proceeds to justify on these grounds the consistent attitude of the British Government, and to remind his countrymen that, had their ideas prevailed in 1861, there could have been no blockade of the Southern coast and the Union could only have been maintained at the cost of hundreds of thousands more lives, if, indeed, it could have been maintained at all.

It is easy, of course, to dismiss Captain Mahan's theory of private property at sea being national in its employment as mere casuistry, but that will not serve. The truth it expresses will remain. We have a moral and indefeasible right at sea as well as on land to prohibit and stop, so far as we can without cruelty or unnecessary hardship, the flow of enemy's commerce, on which her resources for war depend as truly as they do upon armies and fleets. If private men in the face of this admitted right choose to ignore the state of war and still embark their property in commerce, they do so with their eyes open and must not complain of the consequences. Let them keep their property quiet at home and it will not be touched—at least by the sea service.

There still remains to be dealt with the argument upon which our own idealists chiefly rely. It is an argument to which allusion has been made already, but has nothing to do with morality, justice, or humanity. For though it is obvious between the lines that our advocate of reform are as sincerely moved as the Americans by an ideal of Christian progress, Briton-like they do not talk about it. With us such things are felt, not spoken. We prefer to offer material, selfish reasons for the faith that is in us, and consequently our idealists argue that the recognition of the sanctity of private property at sea would be a distinct military advantage to ourselves, and, moreover, as is also usual in such cases, that if we do not seize the opportunity to recognize it now it will not occur again. "I trust," says the Lord Chancellor, referring to President Roosevelt's proposal to have the thing settled at the coming Hague Conference:

> I trust that his Majesty's Government will avail themselves of this unique opportunity. [How familiar is the phrase!] I urge it not upon any ground of sentiment or humanity (indeed, no operation of war inflicts less suffering than the capture of unarmed vessels at sea), but upon the ground that on the balance of argument, coolly weighed, the interests of Great Britain will gain much from a change long and eagerly desired by the great majority of other Powers.

So, then, it is for military reasons that we are to consent to have the teeth pulled upon which we have relied for so many generations, and to "abandon in great measure," as Captain Mahan has put our case, "the control of the sea, so far as useful to war." Let us, then, frankly examine these military reasons which the Lord Chancellor sets forth for they are not at once convincing. Indeed, it is obvious that the Lord Chancellor has not brought to bear upon the subject the profound study of war with which his great predecessor, Lord Hardwicke, enlightened our councils during the Seven Years' War. We might even beg seriously that before he gives the weight of his high reputation and exalted office any further to the movement he would read and re-read that masterly series of letters which the greatest of the Chancellors addressed to the Duke of New-castle and others during the most successful war we ever waged.

The main military or strategical argument that is urged is that, as we have the greatest amount of private property afloat, and rely more than anyone upon commerce for our resources, we stand to lose most by the maintenance of the existing law. "Our merchant marine," says the Chancellor, "is vulnerable in proportion to its size and ubiquity." This is a tremendous assumption, natural enough to one who has made no study of the realities of war; but we may venture to assert that it is one which our naval staff would certainly hesitate to endorse. To point out its fallacy completely would require a whole excursus on the British ideas of commerce protection, and possibly the disclosure of matters which the Admiralty had better keep to itself. But plain sense will suggest difficulties in accepting this very common view. Everyone must know that a cruiser's capacity for destroying commerce is not unlimited. How very limited it is the Chancellor clearly has not well considered. A cruiser can scarcely take more than one ship at once, and to overhaul and ascertain the nationality of a ship takes time. She cannot, moreover, be in two places at once, and the sea is wide. To reach a station where she may safely begin her operations (unless we have entirely lost command of the sea) she will burn coal—she will want plenty to get back again; the time, consequently, during which she can pursue her depredations is very limited indeed. These simple matters, so real to naval officers, are usually ignored by civilians. The broad truth is that if we look at the matter from the point of view of practical warfare, and not pure mathematics, we shall see that there is at least a case for the opposite of the Chancellor's postulate. The greater the bulk of commerce, the more difficult does it become to make any serious impression upon it. The greater the bulk, the larger will be the percentage that is beyond the utmost predatory capacity of the enemy's fleet. Thus it is at least arguable that the invulnerability of the mass sea-borne commerce increases with its bulk and ubiquity. To carry the matter further is impossible in this place. It must suffice to have pointed out that the Chancellor's postulate cannot be swallowed whole until it has been well seethed in salt water. In the process it might entirely change color.

Take, again, another similar argument. "The principal necessities of England's Navy," writes Professor Sheldon Amos, "are to protect her commerce, defend her coasts, and overpower the enemy: it is obvious if the Navy could be relieved of any one of these functions, so much the more disposable it would be for the efficient discharge of the other two." Here, of course, we are even further from salt water than with the Chancellor; but the passage, teeming as it does with error, has been seriously quoted abroad. How do the Professor and those who complacently cite him imagine that we can defend our coasts without defending our trade, or do either without overpowering the enemy? It is all one—all a matter of getting control of the common communications. Unless and until we do that we have not overpowered the enemy, and we have not gone the best way about defending our coasts and commerce. Casual cruising against our commerce we can ignore, if necessary, in the process of getting control, so small nowadays is the reach and capacity of cruisers and so great the bulk of our commerce. As for serious fleet attacks upon it, we can desire nothing better. It is all very well to talk of overpowering the enemy, of seeking out the enemy's fleet and destroying him, but for this he must let you get at him. That was always our great difficulty; and there is no means so good for making him expose himself as attacking his commerce with your fleet and tempting him to attack yours with his. If our commerce were made as sacred from capture as an ambassador it would give little or no relief to our battle fleets, while, on the other hand, if we were denied the right to attack enemy's commerce we should lose the one sure and rapid means of forcing his battle fleet to a decision.

This brings us to the final part of the argument. It is freely contended that while the immunity of sea-borne commerce would greatly relieve the strain of defence, it would scarcely affect our power of attack. The grinding power of offence which we exercised by attack on commerce in the old wars is recognized, or not denied. But it is asserted that since Napoleonic times, when these wars came to an end, the conditions have entirely changed. The change has taken place in two ways. Firstly, by the Declaration of Paris we are no longer able by general capture to prevent the enemy's commerce being carried in neutral ships; and, secondly, it is contended that the vast development of inland communications has made Continental nations practically independent of sea-borne trade—that is, in so far as exerting pressure to compel peace is concerned. Here again we have two of those breezy generalizations which trip so gaily from the pens of international jurists, as though they were not laden and tangled with a nexus of practical considerations, complex and indeterminate to the last degree, and entirely beyond even approximate measurement. They seem airily to neglect the fact that the capacity of neutral shipping and of inland communications is not unlimited, and to ignore the well-known difficulty of forcing trade to flow healthily out of the channels into which it has settled itself. Neutral ships are always fairly well full of their own business, and if you suddenly throw upon them the extra work of even one considerable mercantile marine, they will either be unequal to the task or freights must leap up to a seriously disturbing degree. The case of railways and inland navigation is treated with even a less appreciation of what actually happens in war. The capacity of railways is even less elastic than that of neutral ships. In peace time their carrying capacity, for plain reasons of business, is seldom much beyond the traffic which accrues in supplying the actual necessities of the nation, and to calculate that with the intolerable extra strain that is always thrown upon them by the paramount exigencies of a great war they would still be able to deal with an equivalent of the normal sea-borne traffic is simply to ignore universal experience and the elementary facts of commerce. Even were it possible in any reasonable time to get land communications to bear all their ordinary peace traffic as well as the war traffic and that of the paralyzed mercantile marine, the dislocation of national life and action must at least produce so great a shock to trade, industry, and, above all, credit as to be a strategical blow of the highest order. It is at least a possibility of drastic offence that we, who are so weak, and must always be so weak in the means open to the great military Powers, cannot afford to forego.

I know it is argued by some of our most respected and earnest journals that our position and the peace of the world would gain a real solidity by the sacrifice, and a real motive for the growth of armaments would be removed, because we should thereby demonstrate that our Navy is meant only for defence. But that is a point incapable of demonstration, simply because it is not true. Our Navy is under certain circumstances intended for offence. Such circumstances, happily, are remote, but it is sheer fatuity to think they cannot possibly arise. Not only is no real and crushing defence possible without attack, but in cases where we are the injured party and no redress can be had except by war, then direct offence is necessary. It is a distasteful subject, above all to the higher Liberalism, where the desire to unarm is keenest. But it has to be faced, and must be faced without false sentiment, as Sir William Harcourt faced it in the great debate already cited:

> There is only one security [he said] for a great naval Power: as far as you can and as soon as you can to sweep the enemy from the seas. Not only must we preserve our right to fight against the navy of our enemy, but to capture all the ships it possesses and all the means it possesses by which we may be attacked. It is the legitimate arm of this great Empire—the arm by which we defend our extended Empire. I go a great deal farther. There is no security in war unless we are strong for offence as well as defence.

It is true. We cannot make ourselves stronger for defence or for doing our part in preserving the peace of the world by casting away our most trenchant and well-approved weapon. It was not the custom at King Arthur's Court for his knights to equip themselves for their holy quests by discarding their spears and trusting to shield and dagger.

In conclusion, it is necessary to enter a protest against one other argument, which is too often advanced by the advocates of immunity, and particularly from commercial centres. Failing to see they have involved themselves in a question which is mainly one of strategy and war-plans, and unable to grasp the force of the naval objection, they do not scruple to suggest that the opposition of naval officers arises from their desire for prize-money. It is to be hoped they scarcely grasp how wanton an insult they offer to a great and honorable Service and how deeply the suspicion is resented. No one in touch with the ungrudging devotion of the modern naval officer could believe for one moment that he would permit so sordid a consideration even to color the advice he gave his country on so high a matter. It is intolerable the slander should be repeated as often as it has been. Prize-money has nothing whatever to do with the matter.

Many officers indeed are of opinion that for the good of the Service alone the system should be abolished. There might be cases in time of war, as there were in days gone by, when prize-money might warp a man's sense of duty. Therefore, they say, let it go—to whom you will. What is good for the Service is good enough for us. Chambers of commerce may find difficulty in appreciating the depth and reality of the sentiment. Could they but do so they would never permit the prize-money argument to sully their petitions again. The reason why naval officers urge with heart and soul the retention of the old right of capture is because they know not how to make war without it, nor can any man tell them.

CHAPTER FOUR

Doctrine—the Soul of Warfare

T he core agenda of Julian Corbett's work was to record the evolution of national strategy, through historical case studies that would inform the development of national, strategic doctrine; strategy was national process and must not be left to individual armed services. As early as 1900 he had concluded that treating naval and military history in isolation was fundamentally unsound, as was the construction of strategy by individual armed services. He argued that Britain, a unique global maritime power, needed a distinct strategy based on theoretical understandings of war but shaped by British experience. This experience had demonstrated that Britain had been successful only when it used strategies that combined the army and the navy and had to be recognized in that way. In 1911 Corbett established the distinctive character of British strategy in *Some Principles*; the following year he found an opportunity to examine the expanding field of Official History the following year. His purpose: to secure military recognition of academic history as a suitably "scientific" resource for the Services to use and to secure academic recognition of defense education as valid output for historians.

Through his extensive academic and social network Corbett brought together a panel on naval and military history at the 1912 London International Historical Congress. This gathering was unprecedented—the largest gathering of historians in the world. The congress offered Corbett a stage where he could address both his audiences—the military and academia. He personally organized the naval papers to be presented and secured a venue at the Royal United Services Institute, only minutes from the Admiralty, the War Office, and the Houses of Parliament. The panels were chaired by senior defense figures, including the first sea lord. The combination of international academic recognition and service endorsement as reflected in a panel of civilian and service speakers ensured Corbett's ideas would be taken seriously. The papers formed a self-contained study of the evolution and prospects of naval history as a core element in service education. Corbett's essay on official histories was designed to persuade the Navy that historians who employed sound philosophical methods made history "a treasure house of rich experience" in which naval officers could search for principles. These methods transformed the past from a heap of jumbled facts into "a minc of experience . . . from which right doctrine—the soul of warfare—can be built up."[1] Such transformation was a task for an educated, rather than an experienced, intellect—an academic not an officer.

To make this vision possible, however, the contemporary vogue for Official Histories necessitated reconsidering the Histories' construction. Older wars merited study to provide general insight; recent conflicts offered more directly relevant insights for the next conflict. In analyzing older wars it was essential to avoid unnecessary detail and bring out "general principles which are inseparable from the conduct of all wars." Critically this analysis should include "the deflections of purely military operations which were caused by political exigencies and influences," a possibility when studying older conflicts because no one living would be offended.

To emphasize his contention that British policy was unique, Corbett pointedly dismissed the widely praised German General Staff history of the Seven Years' War, which completely ignored the maritime dimension. His real target was far closer at hand: the continentalist Imperial General Staff, based just across the road, were dreaming German dreams of mass conscript armies and "decisive" theaters. He preferred the methodology of French General Staff: not imposing a specific staff solution but rather seeking to solve particular problems through documentary collections designed to be used by students. Corbett argued that staff histories should seek "the solution of special problems."[2] Most of his audience would have recognized in this argument the methods of the Navy Records Society, in which he was the effective director. General histories of older wars were best left to civilian historians, although he was too modest to cite *England in the Seven Years' War: A Study in Combined Strategy*, the obvious example.

Studies written immediately after modern conflicts needed to be comprehensive, but it was impossible to be wholly frank about political and other external deflections—anything written in the lifetime of those involved would be necessarily limited. These faults rendered such works more "materials for history" than true history itself. Professional historians might be able to make such materials more useful than serving officers.

Corbett emphasized the need for cooperation in any future Historical Section between officers and academics. He was not afraid to admit he needed a helping hand to round out his comprehension of the naval past to ensure he could be an effective resource for education. Historical conclusions based on the balance of evidence and "disciplined judgment" were not intended to resolve "modern technical problems." Problem solving belonged to service experts, but their reports should not violate historical methods. His case study was the use of the past in the *Dreadnought* controversy. Trained historians were competent to assess past practice, a reference to his work on the tactical importance of the three-decked ship at the Trafalgar campaign, and to ensure "false historical conclusions are not used to prove that a particular modern type is either right or wrong."[3] No one in the audience with any grasp of the *Dreadnought* controversy could have been unaware of his targets: Reginald Custance and Cyprian Bridge, already working on the Admiralty Report on Nelson's tactics at Trafalgar, as well as William White and Alfred T. Mahan. In pursuit of a contemporary obsession, criticizing Fisher's *Dreadnought*, all four had failed as historians. To avoid any repetition of this, Corbett favored "free collaboration" between military and scholarly expertise—his relationship with Captain Edmond Slade of the Royal Navy would have been the obvious model or with a historically trained naval officer such as fellow Congress speaker Herbert Richmond.

Britain posed a unique problem for Staff Histories—a problem recognized after flawed attempts to analyze the Russo-Japanese war in separate Army and Navy Historical Sections. The solution was to base the Official History project in the Committee of Imperial Defence (CID) rather than the individual services. The need to separate operational and tactical analysis from grand strategy remained until the British Second World War Official History included a separate series on "Grand Strategy." Corbett's experience writing the CID's confidential history of the Russo-Japanese War led him to conclude that the best method was an analytical narrative, very much the province of a historian. After the success of his books *The Seven Years' War* and *The Campaign of Trafalgar* he was quietly confident his own Official History would transcend such limitations.

Corbett's educational legacy has been contested by other approaches to strategy, defense, international relations, and political thinking. However, these theoretical tools suffer from the same problem he identified in his own military contemporaries' thinking—the dangerous delusion of universal applicability. He saw no purpose in parroting ideas developed in other contexts for other countries. Strategy is an art, and it must be national or alliance based. What works for one country or coalition cannot be assumed to work elsewhere. Corbett used strategic theory to create a British national strategic doctrine; he did not think it would be applicable elsewhere because Britain was unique. He built doctrine from a deep engagement with the national past, which he used to test and evolve the appropriate strategic models and to ultimately create a working overview. He did not offer universal wisdom, or prescriptive advice, even when he did produce "principles," they were qualified as "some," and not "the," and he planned to update them regularly. He insisted that experience took precedence over theory; bland generalizations were no substitute for hard lessons. In his 1905 text, *The Influence of Sea Power upon the War of 1812*, Mahan had taught his own Service one such "hard lesson." He told the USN what had gone wrong in 1812, in searing detail, to ensure the same mistakes were not repeated.

Defense education demands specialist educators embedded within the Service but not necessarily provided by military personnel. Civilians are cheaper, better trained, less engaged in the in-Service issues, and more focused on the civilian direction of war than are those in their military peer group. The civilians' task is to capture, analyze, and deliver the wisdom of the past at every stage of defense education, a role that becomes more important at the strategic level. The history they produce is not written for academic debate, any more than Corbett's was; it serves to educate future decision makers.

STAFF HISTORIES

1913

Of late years there has been a large output of work from the Historical Sections of Naval and Military Staffs, which has wrought a revolution in the study of war history. No historian whose task has brought him in touch with this work can fail to appreciate its value, nor in the care and thoroughness of its methods can we fail to recognise a complete change in the attitude of the Services to history. The underlying cause of the change is not far to seek. It is, primarily at least, due to the sound and philosophical method which the Historical Sections have adopted that has led them directly to an appreciation of the practical living value of history—that has revealed history not as a museum of antiquities, but as a treasurehouse of rich experience.

For I would venture to say that the scepticism as to the practical value of historical study which formerly existed in the Services—and especially in the Naval Service—was mainly due to unsound method. The common procedure was that men, who from their own practical experience had convinced themselves that some particular method or means of conducting war should be adopted, were accustomed to go to such history as was available for facts to demonstrate their preconceived opinion. Their opponents met them with a similar selection of facts, and the inevitable result was a sceptical feeling that history like statistics could prove anything, and with practical men history was brought into contempt. That has now passed away, under the influence of more philosophical methods, and officers no longer look upon history as a kind of dust heap from which a convenient brick may be extracted to hurl at their opponents. They no longer go to it to prove some empirical view of tactics or

Julian S. Corbett, "Staff Histories," in *Naval and Military Essays: Being Papers Read at the Naval and Military Section of the International Congress of Historical Studies*, ed. J. S. Corbett and H. J. Edwards (Cambridge: University of Cambridge Press, 1914), 24. Paper delivered in 1913.

material, or to show that some battle or other was fought in the way they think it ought to have been fought. They go to it as a mine of experience where alone the gold is to be found, from which right doctrine—the soul of warfare—can be built up.

If we were to reduce the change that has taken place to a rough generalisation we might say—that formerly men went to history to prove they were right; now they go to it to find out where they are wrong; or, as it has been well said, they go to history to search for principles, not to prove those which they believe they have already found.

The main question then with regard to Staff Histories is no longer concerned with their value or purpose; it is concerned rather with the best means of producing them, the best means, that is, of getting from them the desired results. And in endeavouring to find a solution we have first to face the fact that these histories are not all in the same category.

A broad distinction will at once suggest itself between histories of bygone wars, waged with material that is now quite obsolete and under conditions that no longer exist, from which we can only derive the broader doctrines; and histories that deal with the wars of yesterday, in which, in spite of the rapid development of material, we seek for closer and more direct light on the wars of to-morrow.

Each class has its own special value and its own facilities of production. As an example of the first class we may take the German Staff History of the Seven Years' War. That shows us at once that the distant standpoint, from which the war is regarded, permits a seizure of its salient features. Unimportant detail disappears and a broad treatment is possible which seems to bring out in bold touches the general principles which are inseparable from the conduct of all wars. From the distant standpoint we are also able to appreciate clearly the deflections of purely military operations which were caused by political exigencies and influences, and to which modern military theory attaches so much importance. For in the case of the older wars there is no longer any reason why such matters should be kept secret. On this point, it is true, this particular history is not quite satisfactory, since it is confined to the continental and European theatre of the war, and the influence of the maritime theatre is ignored.

For the history of the older wars we have also another type of work—a good example of which is Colonel Desbriere's *Projets et tentatives de débarquement aux îles Brittanniques,* 1798–1805, issued under direction of the French General Staff. Here is a work that aims not so much at a history of a particular war as at the solution of a certain war problem; and to do this it proceeds on lines opposite to the type of the German History. So far from seeking mainly by the broad treatment to detach general principles, it offers a complete collection of documents, orders, and statistics from which the solution of the problem may be extracted by close study. But the lucid comment is interwoven which leaves us in little doubt what the correct answer is.

So successful indeed is that work that it seems to point strongly to what is the right use for Historical Sections to make of the older history. It suggests that Historical Sections should not concern themselves with producing regular histories of such wars, but rather should go to them for the solution of special problems—so that the whole experience at our command may be brought to bear on the solution we are seeking.

An additional argument for taking this view is that, for reasons which will be suggested later, it is probable that the production of regular histories of the older wars is more within the province and capacity of civilian historians and may with advantage be left to them.

These considerations, however, do not apply with anything like the same strength to our second category—that is, histories which are required as soon as possible after a war has been fought, such as our own history of the Boer War and the Russian history of the Russo-Japanese War. These necessarily demand the study of the particular war as a whole; for their conspicuous merit is that their object is avowedly to study the mistakes that were made with a view to preventing their recurrence. This leads to an illuminating frankness which is the marrow of real history.

But they labour under two drawbacks. One is, that frankness about political and other external deflections is not entirely possible, since the time has not come when such matters can be laid openly upon the table. The other, that since they are written in the lifetime of the men who fought them there is a tendency to modify criticism. In close connection with this there is a feeling that the history must not only be a Staff History—in the higher sense of an instructional work—but it must also serve as a complete chronicle of the war, in which the part of every unit must have justice done to it, with the result that we are sometimes smothered with a mass of detail acquired at vast labour and expense which has little or no value for the main purpose in hand.

I am not suggesting that these defects can be entirely avoided. Probably time alone can provide the complete remedy. Still it must be said that in the eyes of a professed historian these works are not quite histories, but rather they are—like collections of documents—materials for history. And I trust that I may be pardoned for saying that probably an expert historian—proceeding on the well-known principles of his craft—would indicate ways in which some of these defects could be avoided and by which the book might be rendered much more digestible to a hard-worked officer seeking to improve his knowledge of his profession.

I make this comment with the less diffidence because it is possible to point to an example where the principles I refer to have been followed by an officer who was also a man of letters and an accomplished historian. I mean the official history of the Tel-el-Kebir campaign by the late General Sir Frederick Maurice. The whole affair is dealt with by him in about 100 pages, and I believe it is held to be a very satisfactory and comprehensive account. True, the campaign was short and comparatively simple, but none the less I would submit we may look to this work as a standard of method to be approached as nearly as the subject in hand permits.

Further, I should like to make it clear that in drawing attention to the inordinate length and heaviness of recent Staff Histories we fully appreciate that these defects are the defects of their best qualities. They are due to the conscientious and minute research upon which the narratives are built up and the untiring efforts to be correct and just. They are defects with which every modern historian has to struggle in these days of voluminous material, but they can be overcome by a fuller study of the art of narrative and the art of selection. I do not pretend these things are easy; for usually they are the last qualities to which a professed historian attains after lifelong practice.

These considerations lead naturally to my second point—as to how Staff Histories can best be produced. Here, again, I would distinguish between considerations which apply generally and those which concern a British Staff.

Clearly, if Staff Histories are susceptible of the distinct classification I have indicated, the method of treatment is likely to vary, but in each case the crux seems to be co-operation. Take first the histories of the older wars. Here officers reaching back for their material find themselves on ground that is unfamiliar to them, but quite well known to professed historians. They have to set to work with a mass of purely historical evidence that requires special training for its right handling. The skill can be acquired, and I believe there are few better schools than a historical section, but it takes time, especially if the acquisition is attempted without expert instruction. And here, in justification of my suggestion that these histories are perhaps better left to professed historians, I would venture with deference to offer a few warnings which are addressed mainly to naval officers, partly because most of their history is so old and partly because it seems that military officers, from the nature of their education and the wealth and excellence of their literature, have a much better chance of acquiring the necessary skill and mental attitude, than the peculiar training and occupations of naval officers permit.

If, then, I may be allowed to do so—in no spirit of censure or superiority, but with a genuine desire to assist in the difficult path—I would say that for the unskilled hand endeavouring for himself to elucidate a problem by the experience of the long dead masters there are traps innumerable. Perhaps the best way to make the danger and difficulty clear is by analogy. In the mystery of the sea-craft there is something that sailors call "seamanship," an intangible but necessary equipment which they know it is extremely difficult for civilians to acquire. In its broader sense it is impossible to define or even to explain; but we know that it is something only to be mastered by long service afloat, and that it so completely permeates the whole subject of naval warfare that no civilian writers can hope to avoid grave error without the assistance of naval officers. Those of us at least who have dared to walk upon the waters know well the need of their helping hand.

On the other part, historians have something akin to it—something with which the training of a naval officer leaves him unfamiliar—and we call it "scholarship"; consequently he will sometimes devote his leisure to history with little suspicion that without some equipment in scholarship he will err as seriously as will civilians without seamanship. The one is as essential and as intangible as the other. Scholarship is only to be attained by long and devoted service—by long mental discipline, by regular initiation into the methods of dealing with historical evidence, of tracing it to its sources, of testing their value, and finally of raising upon it conclusions which are as free, as fallible human minds can make them, from preconceived ideas.

But in speaking of conclusions which are within the province of historical scholarship, it is important to make it clear that what is meant are historical and not technical conclusions. While emphatically repudiating any suggestion that the province of historians is merely to collect and marshal facts for officers to deal with, it is equally necessary to insist upon the line beyond which historians should not venture in drawing conclusions, and this line can be drawn very distinctly. It lies between historical conclusions, which depend upon the balance of historical evidence and disciplined historical judgment, and technical conclusions, which are arrived at by applying historical conclusions to the solution of modern technical problems. The first are clearly within the province of professed historians, the second are beyond their province and must be left to experts in the Services. The two spheres can easily be kept apart, and their mutual relations can at the same time be actively preserved, if it be only admitted that, as in naval matters, no technical conclusion is safe without seamanship, so no historical conclusion is safe without scholarship.

To clear the point with a concrete instance, it is submitted that the right type of battleship to-day is a technical conclusion. But on the other hand the determination of the principles which decided the type of battleship in the past is an historical conclusion. With the type to-day the historian has nothing to do, but it is his business to see that false historical conclusions are not used to prove that a particular modern type is either right or wrong.

The practical outcome of these considerations is that there are three ways in which naval history may be produced for staff purposes. The ideal probably is free collaboration between the historical expert and the naval expert. But we may also look for it with confidence from the naval officer who has been at the pains to acquire the elements of historical technique either from professed historians, or by practical work in an

Historical Section; and *vice versa* from the civilian who has had opportunity of learning the lie of the more obvious pitfalls that beset the path of the naval amateur, and who has taken the trouble to master the not very extensive professional literature which deals with the principles of naval warfare.

It remains to inquire—what are the special considerations which apply to the production of Staff History in our own particular case? The greater part of our peculiar war history is the history of what Pitt called "maritime war"—that is, war in which the Army and the Navy are engaged together. This side of the subject has received little attention from any staff and consequently our experience is small. Till quite recent years Historical Sections have had to deal almost entirely with great continental wars, into which the sea factor hardly entered, and consequently their history was dealt with naturally by the military staffs and with excellent results. But were we ever to try to deal with our own war history in this way, it is obvious that serious difficulty would arise. The most pronounced deflections in war are those which naval operations exercise upon land operations and *vice versa*. So far, indeed, do these mutual reactions penetrate a maritime war, when both Services are fully engaged, that it becomes necessary to treat Army and Navy as units of one combined force. How, then, should the history of such wars be produced? The answer seems obvious—by a joint Historical Section formed from both Services. The question forced itself upon us some ten years ago, when the struggle in the Far East confronted us with a great war of the old and almost forgotten type. How was it to be dealt with? Most countries, I believe, began to attack it with two Historical Sections, the one naval and the other military. We ourselves were among the number, but as the preparation of the work revealed how intimately the naval and military operations were entwined it was decided to amalgamate the two branches as one joint section of the Committee of Defence under a single head.

It will be agreed that that was the logical procedure, the method apparently best calculated to emphasise the essential unity of the land and sea forces of an island country and that it was an experiment that had to be tried. But whether the experiment has quite justified itself by success is not so clear. For all the excellent matter which the joint section is producing, for all the care and precision of its method, it leaves, so far as it has gone, an uneasy feeling that it has failed as a work of art. By failing as a work of art I mean it has failed in conveying the impression it set out to convey. Its outstanding characteristic is not a firm hold on the interaction of sea and land. It gives us not so much combined history as naval and military history in strata. We find naval operations arising out of a military situation or closely affecting it have to wait their time till the military narrative is completed, and by the time it is done we have lost the connecting thread. Again, the military narrative has to be broken in order to make room for naval operations that belong logically to a different stage of the general development, and we find with a sense of mental dislocation that we have been forming judgments without all the facts before us.

I would not exaggerate these defects, but any professed historian, practised in the art of marshalling complex narrative, can see that they are there and that they do detract from the value of an otherwise admirable book. What I wish to suggest is that these defects are in no way due to individuals, but that they are due to the system. It used to be thought, and the idea still lingers in continental staffs, that joint-expeditions should have a single commander-in-chief. The idea is logical—even obvious— one of those fallacies which are said to "stand to reason"; but our experience proved it *was* a fallacy and that the only way to work such joint operations was with two co-equal commanders-in-chiefs acting in perfect and loyal harmony. With a single commander-in-chief, experience tells that the needs and limitations of one Service will too often be overridden by those of the other, and it is probable that an analogous process is inseparable from joint historical work.

But even if with a joint section a perfectly equal and smooth co-ordination could be obtained, we cannot escape another drawback. And that is this. The more thoroughly the work is done the more must it result in the student of each Service being harassed with a mass of detail which does not concern him and from which he can profit nothing.

What then is the solution? I would submit that if the art of maritime warfare is to be clearly and profitably treated in historical exposition it must be done either from the sea or from the land. To deal adequately with a maritime war for staff purposes there must be two books and two

Historical Sections. Each book, while preserving its own standpoint, must always keep in view the field of the other. It will deal in detail with the plans and operations of its own Service, but at the same time it will be careful to keep before the eyes of the reader the progress of the operations of the sister Service. They must never be dropped out of the narrative, and with a little of the technical skill which every historian has to exercise they may always be brought into view without obscuring or interrupting the main thread. They need only be given in outline, but they must be given or the true main thread will be lost. And this can be done without difficulty if the two sections work in intimate connection, each freely consulting the other in its special sphere, and each freely communicating to the other its special knowledge. In this way it would seem that the spirit of co-ordination, which means everything to a country like ours, may be fostered and its practical aspects studied far better than in one book. For each Service will be free to elaborate its own detail, and free to develop its own doctrine and at the same time be able to keep it in due subservience with that of the sister Service.

Nor need there be any practical difficulty in securing the necessary harmony of working. Recent experience goes to show that such harmony is readily obtained if both sections are under one roof—precisely as in our old conjunct expeditions it was obtained by both commanders-in-chief sailing in one ship.

That I venture to believe is the solution of the difficulty that has arisen—the difficulty which only experiment could have revealed, and that, I would submit, is the method upon which in the future our Staff History should proceed.

CHAPTER FIVE

The Origins of Modern Naval History

S ir John Knox Laughton (1830–1915), widely regarded as the founding father of modern naval history, died in 1915. Laughton had recruited Corbett to the calling in 1893 when he set up the Navy Records Society, and the two men had remained close thereafter. Their work overlapped; from Laughton Corbett had learned the critical need for sophisticated historical input in the naval debates, from education and training to tactics and strategy. A commission from Laughton's Record Society set Corbett working in the archives. In 1912, when Laughton finally abandoned the leadership of the Record Society and the discipline generally because of increasing age and blindness, Corbett had taken up the challenge of leading British naval history.[1] In 1913, at Corbett's request, Laughton delivered a lecture on naval history at the International Congress of Historical Studies. (See chapter 4 for Corbett's contribution to this event.)

When Corbett came to lecture at King's College London in October 1916, where Laughton had been professor for thirty years, he did so to commemorate a great man and friend and to advance Laughton's vision of an academic future for naval history. It was no accident that the lecture was chaired by Admiral Prince Louis of Battenberg, who had chaired Laughton's 1913 lecture. The occasion, the opening of a naval history library based on books from Laughton's own collection, was not quite what it seemed. The "library" was doubtless no more than a small room in a college that had a multiplicity of such spaces until the 1990s, and there is no record of this "Library" in the college archives. In the event Laughton's books disappeared into the College's general book collection and no Department of Naval History was created. Despite that, King's College has remained the home of academic naval history in Britain. Books with Laughton's signature in them remain in the college library, among them notably his copy of William Laird Clowes' monumental seven-volume *The Royal Navy: A History—From the Earliest Times to 1900*, published around the turn of the twentieth century.

The theme of Corbett's 1916 lecture was Laughton's plan for a Department of Naval History at the college, "a lasting national achievement"; and he took the opportunity to stress the connection between Laughton's careful scholarship and the altogether more ambitious, but less secure, contribution of Alfred Thayer Mahan. He argued that older naval histories, classics like William James' excoriating account of the War of 1812, were a record of effects while the new naval history of Laughton and Mahan looked for causes. This stance was consistent with the current state of historical scholarship and enabled the subject to take a place as part of general history. In universities and colleges, not in naval academies, nations would learn to value the sea and the sea service. Laughton wanted all British and Imperial historians, not just a few specialists, to see the sea.

Corbett stressed Laughton's primacy by referring to a letter in which Mahan had acknowledged how Sir John's work had set his course. Corbett's characterization of Mahan's *The Influence of Sea Power upon History* as a "political pamphlet" was acute, a reflection of Laughton's judgment. Corbett also highlighted Laughton's amazing contributions to the *Dictionary of National Biography*, a late Victorian monument to labor at the bedrock of history. Laughton had written almost all the naval entries in this massive compendium, creating a basic tool for future naval historians—one that Corbett wished to see in a dedicated volume. Laughton's pioneering research had done much to instruct the new subject in archival research methods, while Mahan's work, focused on strategic and tactical questions, had emphasised analytical skills of a very different type. Corbett stressed the need for academic training in historical method to deal with the growing weight of evidence found in documents, published collections, and less reliable sources. As an aside he noted work in progress, including that of Captain Herbert Richmond, RN, a friend and student of both Laughton and Corbett, and stressed the range of work that still required expert treatment from original sources. The audience for such work was the Royal Navy. Corbett suggested the Crimean War (1854–1856) would be "a most informing war on the naval side," but it would be many years before such a study was completed.[2] Other work he noted included editing source materials for the Navy Records Society, the unofficial historical section of the Admiralty War Staff.

Corbett highlighted the need for universities to teach naval history and ensure the wider public recognized the critical role of sea power and the Royal Navy in national history. His point has become more pressing as the passing decades have seen a serious decline in public recognition and academic investigation of naval history. The projected department would produce the academics needed to educate the Royal Navy and establish the basis for education and doctrine development through a combination of historical methods and specialist naval knowledge to recover and digest the past in the broad context of general history. The department would be the intellectual equivalent of a dockyard, the base for the fleet's thinking and the key to sustained development. For the present-minded naval men in the audience Corbett stressed that experience derived from the war now in progress would not replace that of other conflicts. When he wrote "a great war does not kill the past, it gives it new life," Corbett was already developing themes that would dominate his Official

History. He was anxious to demonstrate that the current existential total war, which Britain was waging with mass conscript armies, was absolutely unique and wholly at odds with national practice across three centuries. It was definitely not the model for the future.

THE REVIVAL OF NAVAL HISTORY

October 1916

As a subject for a lecture in memory of the late Professor Sir John Laughton "The Revival of Naval History" naturally suggested itself. We are all conscious that there has been a revival, and that naval history is something different from what it was a generation ago; different in its method of treatment and different in the position it has won.

Without disparaging the good work done by men as James and Beatson in the past—and perhaps there is a tendency to think of their careful work too lightly, since it is undeniable they did not satisfy the standards of our own time—they dealt almost entirely with effects and we want causes too. Their specialization was too rigid for us; we are not content without more coordination with the sister subjects. We want, in fact, to see Naval History take its new place as part of a General History. Above all, we desire to have it based on sound and critical study of all relevant authority. It is the movement in this direction what we mean by the Revival of Naval History and it is of this movement that Laughton was the initiator.

True it is that in public opinion, the revival is associated more generally with another name. It is Admiral Mahan who is commonly regarded as the real pioneer; but it appears that this was not his own view of the origins. We have his own statement to the effect that if there had been no Laughton there would probably have been no Mahan. That fact is, I

Julian S. Corbett, *Laughton Memorial Lecture*, Corbett papers, London: National Maritime Museum, CBT 4/5. Paper delivered at King's College, London, October 4, 1916.

think, hardly appreciated beyond a few of the late Professor's colleagues; but I think this is the time and place to make it more widely known. Good reason as Laughton had to be proud of such a follower, he seldom spoke of it. But once, not long before his death, he placed in my hands a letter from Admiral Mahan—a handsome, generous letter—in which the great American writer said how much he owed to Laughton's inspiration. Many years ago—somewhere back in the 'eighties—Laughton read a paper at the United Service Institution on the value of history to naval officers. Strange as it may seem now, it was then quite a novel idea. The Journal of the Institution in which the lecture was printed came into the hands of Mahan, then a captain, who had never so much as thought of history—so he says; but so deeply impressed was he with Laughton's views, that he there and then decided to take up the study. That is the story of the conception of "The Influence of Sea-Power" as told by the author himself in the letter I read—a letter which honoured both sender and receiver.

The results we all know. In 1891 the book which Laughton had inspired appeared, and the effect was almost magical. For the first time Naval History was placed on a philosophical basis. From the mass of facts which had hitherto done duty for Naval History, broad generalisations were possible. The ears of statesmen and publicists were opened, and a new note began to sound in world politics. Regarded as a political pamphlet in the higher sense—for that is how the famous work is best characterised—it has few equals in the sudden and far-reaching effect it produced on political thought and action.

If I speak of it as a political pamphlet, pray believe that I do so in no mood of disparagement. In its line it is unequalled, but as a great historical synthesis it was undoubtably premature. And this, while paying full homage to the merit and the power of the work, must be fully understood if we are to do justice to Laughton's part, and if we would know where the revival of Naval History stands to-day.

Mahan's work was premature because the facts on which his generalisations could have been securely based were not ascertained when he wrote; large sections of them still unstudied. The wonder is that Mahan could build as well as he did on a foundation so insecure. Laughton at that time was probably the only man who knew how insecure they were—of how little value, how defective, how misleading were most of the books on which Mahan had to rely. The scholar in Laughton forbade his making any such attempt as that in which Mahan almost miraculously succeeded. So while Mahan with real skill and daring was building his castle on the sands, Laughton was digging down to bed-rock. Quietly, devotedly, without ostentation and for long without recognition, he was opening up the foundations and preparing the material for a greater and more enduring structure. The completion of that work is one of the tasks that lie before the Department of Naval History, of which it is hoped that the new Laughton Library is but the first stone. If, happily, the Department materialises, let us see that Laughton's spirit inspires its work as it inspired Mahan, and there can be little doubt of success.

If any should falter in the laborious research that is still to be done, let him think of Laughton in obscurity, turning out article after article for the *Dictionary of National Biography*, without assistance and with ungrudging labour, while other men gathered the fruits. It is a noble monument for any man to have left behind him—too noble to be left beyond the reach of students. I know nothing that could ease the work that lies before us so much as the publication of that great series of naval biographies in a separate work. It was Laughton's keen desire that this should be done, for as a practical worker he knew the difference between having such a guide at one's elbow, and having to break off to find it in a Library. He has left behind him full notes and instructions for the purpose—the fruit of his riper years and study, which would greatly enhance the value of his articles, and especially of those earlier ones which he wrote in the days when access to the best material was a struggle in itself, and when some of it could not be reached at all. Could the publishers of the great dictionary see their way to putting all this new learning within our reach, and so to fulfilling the earnest wish of the man who worked for them so well and so faithfully, they would be adding more than perhaps they know to the debt the nation already owes them.

Now, let us see what remains to be done. It is only possible to indicate it briefly, for there is so much crying out for the labourers in both Laughton's way and Mahan's.

In all higher schools of history—schools, that is, in which we seek to train historians—it is agreed we should begin with the art and mystery of handling the material. Here there are still vast jungles to clear, a wide field for training where students could learn their trade practically. The masses of naval documents that have accumulated in the country are very large, and for the most part they are uncharted. This material lies in several different places, the chief of which are the Public Record Office, the British Museum, the Oxford and Cambridge Libraries, and in printed collections such as those contained in the Reports of the Historical MSS Commission, the Navy Records Society, and similar publications. But there is no way by which you can tell quickly what there is in any of those treasure houses which bears upon the subject or period you wish to study. My own stand-by has always been Laughton's biographies, which are invaluable for giving a lead, but much has become accessible since they were written, and there is, of course, a good deal of ground which they do not cover. What is wanted is a systematic bibliographical hand-book by which everyone can find his way without the uncertainty and the loss of time which preliminary wandering and reconnaissances now entail.

In the Public Record Office, for instance, which is the richest store, there lie a wealth and continuity of record such as perhaps few other subjects and no other country can boast; but the process of making their acquaintance is still a matter of much labour, and not a little luck, in spite of what the slender staff of the Office has been able to perform. They lie there, like other official records, just as they came from the Department—arranged for departmental and not for historical purposes, and until a student has thoroughly mastered the departmental system he cannot tell with certainty where to look for what he wants or whether it is there at all. An exhaustive study of these records, and a clear account of them is one of the chief needs if the revival of Naval History is to be carried on as it should be. This is work admirably adapted to the training of advanced students—work which they can feel is not merely drill, but an operation indispensable to the advancement of learning. It would be long before this field was exhausted, for the same work is required for the other collection of material, whether in MS or printed. This is particularly the case with the Reports of the Historical MSS Commission. For lack of some means of finding what is interred in them, the formidable array of volumes at present is more like a cemetery than a treasure-house. To a great extent this difficulty will soon be mitigated by the issue of a general index, but for the specialist probably something more will be required if that vast field is to be as easy of access as it deserves to be.

So much, then, as an indication of the spade work that lies immediately to hand. Let us now get to the crops that we hope may be raised in due time by the tillers. There are, in the first place, large gaps in the long story of our Navy and its achievements that require filling. Some, like the Dutch Wars and the War of the Austrian Succession, are being worked at by competent hands. There may be others of which I do not know. But at present we have blanks for the War of the League of Augsburg and the whole period from the War of American Independence down to 1815. There is also the Crimea, a most informing war on its naval side, a side on which it has never been studied all that adequately. All that great vineyard is practically still untilled—I mean untilled according to the standard which the Revival demands. It has never been properly worked with the original authorities, or with an eye to the relation of naval policy and operations to the military and political history of the period. All that, of course, is work for the master, but between this an apprentice work with the authorities, on which the student may whet his teeth, there lie two other fields in which the journeyman historian may ripen his powers and advance the goal of producing great history.

First, there is the kind of work for which the Navy Records Society exists. As Archives are studied—private or public—groups of documents will be found that richly deserve publication. The editing of such collections is not only a service to the cause—it is invaluable as a means of training, and in this way the commencing historian can step safely from the student stage into the confines of production. Nor need he doubt a welcome if he has the goodwill and the preliminary training.

The second field affords a path for further advance, and it is one of singular attraction. I mean naval biography. When the aspirant begins to feel his wings, there is nothing upon which he can so hopefully test his powers. There is no more absorbing labour, no form of historical writing is so free from technical difficulty, and none calls more loudly for willing and capable hands. It is not too much to say that, with a few exceptions, there are no satisfactory lives of the great masters of the sea. All, or nearly all, require re-writing, in line with modern standards, and from all the new material that has become accessible. From Blake to Collingwood there is scarcely one who has a monument which as the country owes him. I need only mention such names as Norris, Anson, Howe, Kempenfeldt, and St. Vincent.

And let us not underestimate the seriousness of this kind of history. I believe it is one of the aims of the proposed Department to carry on the work of bringing home to the nation at large what it owes to the sea and the Navy; and there is no surer way to the heart of the nation than through the life-story of its heroes. For this purpose biographical history is probably even better adapted than the larger and more ambitious narratives. They appeal rather to the makers of public opinion than to public opinion itself. In this direction of nourishing a healthy national sentiment, much, of course, has already been done. We have seen the effect of it conspicuously in the past two years. If anyone would question the stimulating influence of Naval History, there is something to which we may point with confidence. The patience with which the country bore the apparent inactivity of the Fleet in those early days of the war was quite a new experience. The months of seeming failure during which the Navy was engaged in those prolonged and world-wide operations which finally swept the enemy's cruisers from the seas were never so loyally endured before. Contrast the quiet of that time with the querulous complaints of the old wars, with the angry impatience which Hawke at last stifled in Quiberon Bay, and even as late as the Crimean War with the uninstructed hustling of the Baltic Fleet. In this war there has been nothing of the kind. From the first day every publicist, with full understanding and complete conviction, has tried to teach what he had learned from the revival of Naval History, and the nation listened with results of incalculable value to those who had to direct the war.

But it is not only with public opinion that the Department may hope to be concerned. The highest aim of all—and I think we may call it so—will be to open more widely to the Royal Navy itself the treasures of its rich experience, to bring naval officers more intimately into touch with the ideas, the work, and the policy of the men who formed their matchless tradition. The great chiefs of the past are the only masters from whom they can learn, and it is only the historian who can bring them together. Naval History is the great book of naval memory, and the experience has shown that without special historians, well trained and organised, the book would remain sealed. Volumes of it are still sealed, and it will be the first aim of the new Department to open them so that he who runs may read.

It is, of course, the technical, specialised side of Naval History that chiefly fixes our attention. I fear it is too often regarded as having no wider significance. I mean that, speaking generally, it is a subject with which the general historian regards himself as but little concerned. I would submit that that is an error and the cause of much erroneous judgment, even in our best histories. The tendency is to survey the field from the military and the political points of view, and to miss the striking and comprehensive new outlook which is almost always to be obtained from the sea. It seldom fails to give a fresh and clearer light; and sometimes to view a European situation from the quarter-deck of a flagship at sea is little short of a revelation. After all, for an island race and a maritime Empire, it is the sea that binds all its history together; it is the connecting link between all its aspects—political, military, even economical. It is even more, for Naval History is the main binding link that unifies world history. The general historian, then, cannot afford to neglect it, and he is the poorer for that link never having been forged for him. Most of us, I think, who have made Naval History our study could name many trite criticisms which pass from historian to historian, but which will not stand a breath of salt wind. But the trouble is that the general historian cannot get to sea—too often there is no boat—and he has neither time nor skill to build one for himself. So he stays ashore and sees as much as he can. Well, to-day, I hope we are inaugurating a new dockyard which will in time supply a full fleet of the craft that are wanted. We may hope that it will lead to Naval History being no longer regarded merely as a specialist subject. We may hope it will be regarded as indispensable by the general historian as it pours new blood into the old body, and new wine into old bottles, and if some of them are burst in the process there will be no call for tears.

Still, our real love, our driving enthusiasm, will always be on the specialist side, and in this connection there is something further to be said, something which I feel must be pressing on many minds, both in the

Service and out of it. Particularly, I think, to naval officers it must seem that the events in which they are taking part are so tremendous, so novel, so far beyond all previous experience, that nothing that went before can ever count again. There are few, perhaps, even among those most devoted to the practical value of history—I mean its actual value for war direction and Service training—who have been entirely free from this discouragement. Still, in our better moments we know that it is not so; that however great the apparent changes, the past can never lose its value. I would say, then, as my last word: Do not be discouraged by the present. It may seem a catastrophe which renders all that went before insignificant and not worth study for men of action. Let us remember that great wars always had this effect at the time. While we are close to the stupendous event it seems like a flood that has gathered up and swept away everything on which the old lore rested. But it is not so. As time gives us distance we see the flood only as one more pool in the river as it flows down to eternity, and the phenomena of that pool, however great it may be, cannot be understood unless we know the whole course of the river and the nature of all the tributary streams that have gone to make its volume. No, a great war does not kill the past, it gives it new life. No moment, then, could be more opportune than the present for a Department of Naval History to start its career, and no moment could promise a greater certainty of making the revival of Naval History a lasting national achievement.

CHAPTER SIX

Defending Sea Power

In 1907 Corbett set out his position on maritime belligerent rights in an essay that helped to limit the damage done to British strategic power at the Second Hague Convention and influence the decision not to ratify the 1911 Declaration of London. However, the subject resurfaced early in 1915, in a new, more pressing form. German propaganda, recognizing the negative impact of unrestricted submarine warfare and indiscriminate mine laying, excused it by claiming their forces were resisting British "navalism," which they characterized as a great threat to world peace. The German propaganda effort targeted German and Irish populations in the United States and their political representatives. British propaganda in the United States had been quick to highlight the threat of German militarism and Germany and argued "Navalism" was a moral equivalent. Corbett wrote his first propaganda essay, "The Spectre of Navalism" in late April 1915, before the sinking of the *Lusitania* on May 7. Early in 1917 the Foreign Office commissioned him to write "The League of Peace and a Free Sea," which was printed in New York for an American audience. Both were written in two days, amidst other pressing tasks, yet they were serious essays, far more sophisticated than the normal run of British propaganda. Corbett effectively rewrote the history of the Royal Navy, turning it into a morally acceptable, nonaggressive global constabulary run by a benign *Pax Britannica*.

These papers and the rising challenge of the United States exemplified by the 1916 Naval Program prompted Corbett to reexamine the bases of British power. A public lecture in late 1917 contained his most expansive thinking on the future of the British Empire: The empire depended on command of the sea and must make that command appear suitably benign to avoid the danger that such great strength arouse the opposition of an irresistible coalition. British sea power would only be palatable if it could resist the siren call of protectionism, a threat already apparent in 1917. He accepted that the war would change the empire, imagining a future "Sea Commonwealth," a looser federation of nations. There was nothing especially radical in this argument. He had publicly advanced the concept of "a democratic, autonomous commonwealth" back in 1900.[1] Now he envisaged the Dominions and India would take a more prominent role in external policy, but mutual dependence on sea power would ultimately resist centrifugal forces within the empire. While some things had not changed, the sea was just as much "all one" as it had been for the pre-war Royal Navy, but now the sea power needed to secure the empire could only be sustained "by a united effort of the whole organism." The same mutual concession, sympathy, and restraint that were required by the commonwealth would have their place in relations with the wider world after the war.[2]

This lecture was written at the same time as "The League of Nations and the Freedom of the Seas," Corbett's final propaganda piece, with which it shares themes and insights.[3] In this lecture Corbett joined a number of prominent Liberals trying to shape British opinion on the League of Nations idea advanced by President Woodrow Wilson. In Wilson's 1917 The Fourteen Points, his original concept "Freedom of the Seas" made the abolition of maritime belligerent rights "an essential condition of such a League." However, no justification had been offered for this position. These pre-war ideals ignored the realities of war before 1914, to say nothing of the experience of unrestricted submarine warfare.

In peace all seas are free, and if the League achieved its ultimate aim—preventing war—the question of belligerent rights would never arise. But this was hardly likely. The advocates of freedom wanted to abolish the right of belligerents to stop commercial shipping on the high seas and to seize ships belonging to enemy states or those of neutrals found to contain contraband destined for the enemy. However, these rights were as critical to maritime strategy as the right to occupy territory was to land warfare. Maritime strategy was not just a question of navies fighting navies; without economic warfare, sea power would be toothless against an enemy's population and Britain would be disarmed. Corbett warned that Britain would not tolerate this development. Further, the maritime belligerent rights would be critical to making a League "an effective instrument for peace." Economic sanctions would be the easiest and most bloodless method of disciplining aggressors. The current state of the Russian economy suggests they still are.

Corbett found support for his views in Wilson's recent change of emphasis. Wilson's original pronouncement called for the sea to be open for "the common unhindered use of all the nations of the world," but his message to Congress of January 9, 1918, was rather different. The strategic realities of being a belligerent had obliged Wilson to accept that belligerent rights would be essential to enforce League authority.

As Corbett suggested, Wilson's original program would have placed the future of the world in the hands of aggressive military powers like Germany. In the current total war, old-fashioned neutrality simply did not exist. The only remedy was a League with the power to coerce recalcitrant states, and to this end it must be disassociated from notions of complete Freedom of the Seas so that the Maritime powers could uphold the rights of small powers against military aggression.

The case of Belgium, Germany, and Britain in 1914 must have been in his mind as he wrote.

While Corbett set out a strong case, his deeper purpose was skillfully obscured. A League, with full naval powers, would be a powerful force for stability and would bind many nations to protect the interests of both smaller and larger states. Such a League would support the status quo, which would suit a satiated imperial state like Britain: within a functioning League of Nations the British Empire could build coalitions against aggression and other threats to peace.

THE LEAGUE OF NATIONS AND THE FREEDOM OF THE SEAS

1918

The conception of a League of Nations in the shape it has taken during the past few years is marked by a feature which distinguishes it from all its predecessors. For the first time it appears to be assumed that Freedom of the Seas, or, in other words, the abolition of belligerent rights afloat, is an essential condition of such a League, and that the two ideas are inseparable, an assumption which carries the scope of recent proposals distinctly beyond the limits of those to which the seventeenth and eighteenth centuries gave birth.

None of those schemes ever gathered strength to rise from the ground, yet none of them ever burdened itself with such a load as those of the present day are expected to carry. Indeed Freedom of the Seas in the ordinary acceptance of the term is more than a load. A frank examination of what it connotes will show that it must be a spoke in the wheels which in all probability would prevent any conceivable machinery of a

---

Julian S. Corbett, "The League of Nations and the Freedom of the Seas," pamphlet (Oxford: Oxford University Press, 1918).

League from acting with effect. Once formed, a League of Nations may be charged with the definition of belligerent rights at sea and with control of their exercise, but without them it cannot be an effective instrument for peace.

Striking as the new development is it has received too little attention. It has been allowed to slip in almost without comment, and few, if any, of those who of late have been publicly discussing the subject have stopped to inquire why the new feature has intruded itself at this particular juncture. Its credentials are not asked for. Yet obviously its sudden appearance needs explanation if we are to obtain a clear understanding of the trend of opinion as it exists to-day.

The explanation is not far to seek. A glance at the history of the whole movement reveals it at once. It is that the more recent development of the old idea of a League of Nations is the result of a fusion of two schools of thought. The older one, whose object was a league to prevent war, culminated in the Holy Alliance. The newer one is that which grew up after the failure of the Holy Alliance had led men to despair of finding a means for the prevention of war. The new school, whose harvest was the Declaration of Paris and the Geneva and Hague Conventions, sought the more modest goal of mitigating the horrors of war. It is to this school of thought and not to the older one that the idea of Freedom of the Seas belongs. It indeed represents the high-water mark of what may be called the Hague school. It is the creed of its most advanced and enthusiastic advocates.

Naturally these men were also among the most earnest and convinced advocates of the revived movement for a League of Nations. Their support was needed to give it life. The price of their support was the incorporation of their special policy in the new programme. The price was gladly paid; but, at first, it certainly was not measured. The failure to diagnose the full meaning of Freedom of the Seas, and the even deeper failure to penetrate the actualities of Naval Warfare, prevented men observing how far the two conceptions were incompatible, if not mutually destructive.

As every one knows, Freedom of the Seas is an expression very loosely used, and with many shades of meaning, but for practical purposes it is enough to fix its content, as conceived by those who imported it into the programme for a League of Nations. The moment we endeavour to do this we are confronted by a paradox. It is obvious that Freedom of the Seas can only relate to a state of war. In time of peace all seas are free. Since the middle of the nineteenth century, when the Baltic and Black Seas were finally thrown open to commerce, there has been no *mare clausum*, and except for such international regulations as have been agreed upon for the safety and facility of navigation, all men are free to pass the seas at their pleasure. It is only in relation to a state of war that there are any restrictions. If then a League of Nations can attain its object in preventing war the question of Freedom of the Seas does not arise. As an article in the programme it is redundant and paradoxical.

The truth is that even the most devoted and sanguine advocates of a League of Peace realize that a complete extinction of war by that means is not to be expected. It is more than can be believed—at least until human nature has mellowed much farther—that all the nations of the earth will bind themselves never to go to war for any cause whatever, or entirely to abandon force as a means of defending themselves against attack. There must arise cases in which a League of Nations could not prevent war, and would not deem it just to prevent it; and it is presumably to meet such exceptional cases that Freedom of the Seas has become attached to the League of Nations. The intention doubtless is at once to mitigate the severity of the struggle as between the intractable belligerents and prevent the contest interfering with those who are no party to it. If this were the end of the proposed restriction nothing but good could come of it, and it would in no way be incompatible with the active existence of a League of Nations; but we have only to examine the actualities of Naval Warfare and the effect which Freedom of the Seas would have upon them to see that it is very far from the end. Its effect would reach much farther.

As used by its most pronounced advocates, Freedom of the Seas denotes the abolition of the right of capturing private property afloat. They would deny, to belligerents, not only the admitted right to capture neutral property under the law of blockade and contraband, but would also make the trade of the belligerents equally immune, either altogether or in so far as it was not contraband—that is to say, that no matter how fiercely navies contend peaceful merchants and fishermen shall be free to go about their business as though no war were in progress.

What such a revolution would mean to Naval Warfare is clearly not recognized, presumably because of the obscurity which for landsmen has always surrounded it. No such curtailment of belligerent rights has ever been suggested for the land. It is obvious to every one that if in time of war peaceful merchants and husbandmen were allowed to go their way unmolested by requisitions and free to pass where they would, armies could obtain no results. Even if battles could be fought at all, they could lead to nothing. Battles are fought not for their own sake or merely to destroy the enemy's forces. Their ultimate object is the power which the destruction of the enemy's means of resistance gives for so paralysing his national life that he has no choice but to submit. If non-combatants and private property were immune from interference the nation could not be coerced nor the fruits of victory garnered.

With the less familiar contests on the sea, this has never been so self-evident. To the great majority of landsmen, Naval Warfare seems a far-off struggle in which fleets contend in defence of their coasts and cruisers prowl for booty. It is not generally understood that fleets exist mainly to give those cruisers liberty of action against the enemy's commerce, nor that, unless the cruisers can push their operations so far as actually to choke the enemy's national life at sea, no amount of booty they may get will avail to bring the war to an end. It is only by the prevention of enemy's commerce that fleets can exercise the pressure which armies seek, in theory or practice, to exercise through victories ashore; and it is only by the capture and ability to capture private property at sea that prevention of commerce can be brought about. Without the right to capture private property, Naval battles become meaningless as a method of forcing the enemy to submit. Without that right a Naval victory can give nothing but security at home and the power of harrying the enemy's undefended coasts—a form of pressure which no one would care to sanction in these latter days.

It comes then to this—that if Freedom of the Seas is pushed to its logical conclusion of forbidding altogether the capture and destruction of private property at sea, it will in practice go far to rob fleets of all power of exerting pressure on an enemy, while armies would be left in full enjoyment of that power. The balance of Naval and Military power, which has meant so much for the liberties of the world, would be upset, and the voice of the Naval Powers would sink to a whisper beside that of the Military Powers. If this is the forbidding situation to which a League of Nations is to lead—and there is no avoiding it if it is to be clogged with full Freedom of the Seas—how can it be expected that the Great Naval Powers will consent to become parties to it? Yet it is amongst those Powers that are found the most weighty and convinced advocates of a League of Nations. Without their cordial support such a League can never be formed, and that is one reason why, if we persist in coupling the League with Freedom of the Seas, we lay upon it a load it can never lift.

But it is not the only reason. For even if we assume that the League could be formed with this difficult condition attached to it, it would still find itself deprived of the most effective means of attaining its end. All schemes for a League of Nations contemplate some form of sanction by which recalcitrant Powers can be coerced, and of all these sanctions the one that is at once the most readily applied and the most immediate and humane in its action is to deny to the offender the Freedom of the Seas, to pronounce against him a sea interdict. To kill, or even seriously to hamper, a nation's commercial activity at sea has always been a potent means of bringing it to reason, even when national life was far less dependent on sea-borne trade than it is now. At the present time, when the whole world has become to so large an extent possessed of a common vitality, when the life of every nation has become more or less linked by its trade arteries with that of every other, the force of an oecumenical sea interdict has become perhaps the most potent of all sanctions. It is, moreover, one that can be applied without inflicting the inhumanities which other forms of coercion entail. For a League, therefore, whose object is to make an end of the inhuman practice of war it is a sanction which it would be folly to deny itself. Yet if absolute Freedom of the Seas is to be a fundamental article of its constitution that sanction cannot be applied. There would still, of course, remain the sanction of non-intercourse, but without the full sea interdict it would lose more than half its force, and often be too slow and weak in its action to be effective. In too many cases the only trustworthy sanction would still be open war, in which armies alone could bring vital pressure to bear.

To bring the truth of this view home to those who are unfamiliar with the mystery of sea-power is no easy task. To many it will seem to be no more than an obscurant clinging to the past with which they are resolved to break; and naturally enough, when we remember how often opposition to human progress is little else. But in this case the charge of mere obscurantism will not hold. The latest expressions of considered opinion are too weighty and too sagacious to be so easily dismissed. The reality or the objection to fettering a League of Nations with absolute Freedom of the Seas has recently been recognized by a high authority whom no one can suspect of obscurantism. President Wilson, in his original pronouncement for a League of Nations, described his aim as 'a universal association of nations to maintain inviolate the security of the highway of the seas for the common unhindered use of all the nations of the world'. The high seas were to be open to all, in war as in peace, at all times and under all conditions. But that was in the early days of the war, when men had not yet had driven home to them what sea-power actually meant for the cause of peace and freedom and for the punishment of international criminality. In his message to Congress delivered on January 8, 1918, his attitude was profoundly modified. He then took occasion to utter an implicit warning that the original position of the promoters of a League of Nations which he had voiced on the previous occasion was incompatible with their aim. The substance of the message was a Peace programme, and its second article provided for 'absolute freedom of navigation upon the seas outside territorial waters alike in peace and in war, *except as the seas may be closed in whole or in part by international action for the enforcement of international covenants*'. The declaration is perfectly clear. The official policy of the United States is that the old belligerent rights at sea must be retained as essential to the executive ability of the League.

Obviously it must be so. For if those rights were abolished the Sea Powers as such could do nothing to enforce the will of the League. The executive force would lie almost entirely with the Military Powers, and the result of such unequal executive capacity cannot be contemplated with equanimity. It is too well known that the weight of a voice in the council chamber is not determined by reason alone, but in a much higher degree by the force behind it. The Naval Powers, bound hand and foot with the Freedom of the Seas, could speak, but they could not act, and inevitably the councils of the League would be dominated by the Military Powers. Is it credible that in the existing state of human progress a League of Nations under such conditions could make for the sanctity of covenants, the rights of small nations, and the peace of the world? Clearly it is not, and no less clear is it that if we are in earnest for a League of Peace we must concentrate on that end, and not dissipate energy in trying to achieve a wholly distinct aim at the same time. To strive for a League of Peace is to strive to prevent war; to strive for Freedom of the Seas is to admit war and strive to mitigate its terrors. Let us cease to confuse the two ends. Let us determine which line of endeavour we mean to follow, and pursue it with singleness of purpose and undivided effort. It will not be easy. It is to the interest of the Military Powers to confuse the two tracks. They will, undoubtedly, use every device to keep them confused, for only by fostering the unhappy confusion which well-meaning men have hastily introduced can they destroy the balance between Naval and Military Powers, and so become the arbiters of the destinies of their weaker neighbours.

Above all should these smaller nations beware of putting themselves in line on this question with the Military Powers. The temptation is great. Their sufferings as neutrals during the present war have been so severe that their tendency is to snatch at the first means that seems to promise relief in the future. Their troubles are directly traced to the extension of belligerent interference upon the sea to which new developments in war conditions have inevitably led, and it is naturally in Freedom of the Seas they see the only remedy. But in truth their sufferings at sea are only a symptom of the underlying cause. The fundamental difficulty is that the vitality of nations has become so much a common vitality that no nation can fully enjoy a state of peace while other nations are at war. Neutrality as it formerly existed has ceased to be possible, and Freedom of the Seas would be only an alleviation, not a cure. The only real remedy is a League of Nations which would prevent war, but a League of Nations could not permit neutrality as a right—any more than by the English common law a citizen had the right to stand aside when a criminal was being pursued. Except in case of special dispensation all would have to join in enforcing the sea interdict, and all would be in a state of war with the recalcitrant Power.

Whether, then, a League of Nations were formed or not small nations would not see the end of suffering or sacrifice, even if it were possible by a stroke of the pen to abolish so old and well-established a practice as capture at sea. On the other hand, if no League could be formed, or, being formed, could not be made effective, their condition would be more precarious than ever. For without belligerent rights at sea the Naval Powers would be without means to protect them, and they would be at the mercy of the Military Powers with no one to whom they could turn in time of trouble.

For the Minor Powers there is only one escape from the miseries of war, and that is an effective League of Nations. The policy which, in common with all men of goodwill, they must pursue is to see it accomplished, to remove everything that is likely to prove a stumbling block, and to permit nothing which may cripple its vigour when it comes to life. The seas our ship will have to pass are stormy and full of shoals, and of this we may be sure, there is little hope of her avoiding wreck if she is made to labour with this perilous deckload of Freedom of Seas. If it is our real desire to bring her safely to port it must be jettisoned—and the sooner and more completely it is done the better.

Only in this way can we cease to confuse the issue. The all-important end is to get a League into being. Until it is a living fact we cannot tell what form it will take or how much of humanity it will embrace, and until we know these things we cannot tell how far the preservation of belligerent rights at sea, or to what extent their control by the League, will make for the success of the Great Cause.

CHAPTER SEVEN

Selling Naval History, 1919–22

D uring the First World War Corbett reinforced his connections across the dramatically expanding defense sector. He hoped these connections would help him complete his long-term project: establishing the history of war, including naval history, as an academic discipline in a major university. Doing so would ensure the subject had the vitality needed to support advanced naval education and doctrine development. But by 1922 Corbett needed to hand over the task to a new generation—he was past retiring age, in poor health, and desperately trying to complete the British Official History of naval operations and Grand Strategy in the First World War. Although the demanding schedule of managing and writing the Official Histories left him little time for this project, Corbett always tried to exploit opportunities that arose to sustain the place of naval history in the academic environment. Despite the heavy official work schedule, his dedication to history did not suffer. During the war he kept the Navy Records Society alive, provided public lectures at the University of London and the Historical Association, and delivered the first two sets of the Lees-Knowles Lectures at Cambridge University in 1915 and 1917.

Although he did not live to continue his work on strategic history, which had ended in 1910 with *The Campaign of Trafalgar*, in the 1921 Creighton Memorial Lecture Corbett left a vital statement of his evolving sense of how naval history should function as a bridge between academic and service contexts. It was his only major postwar public lecture and was delivered in the Great Hall at Kings College London on the evening of October 11, 1921. With the First Lord of the Admiralty in the Chair, the lecture attracted a large audience of both academic historians and serving officers. The occasion was both a showcase for naval history and an opportunity to address the leaders of the discipline. Despite having no time to write something new, Corbett accepted an invitation to speak. He reused a lecture originally produced for the Naval War Course in 1910 that dealt with the naval war after Trafalgar, suitably reworking it to make the academic case for naval history.

With the civilian head of the Navy sitting alongside him, Corbett stressed the need for a "School of Naval History" to continue his work, citing the period between Trafalgar and Waterloo as a "trackless desert" for students. The subject he had chosen was relatively recent and offered a "striking analogy" with the Great War. Focusing on the defense of floating trade he stressed that "naval" history needed to encompass all national activity at sea. He blamed the separation of maritime history into naval and commercial branches for the failure of mainstream historians to address the subject. This divide remains to be traversed almost a century later.

Corbett's message was simple and subversive. Continental strategists, obsessed with concentration and decision, would judge the British war effort between 1805 and 1812 as weak and inconclusive, as violating sound strategic principles. Yet Britain survived, prospered, and funded the coalition that finally destroyed Napoleon. This use of irony was a direct attack on the arguments of continentally minded soldiers, and it elevated the futile slaughter on the "Western Front" as the focal point of the conflict. The war had hardened Army khaki continentalism into unthinking dogma, so Corbett turned to history—the recent slaughter on the Western Front—to recover the reality of British strategy, which represented everything his strategic teaching had opposed. His intellectual power and drafting skill constructed an argument that could not be refuted by simpletons or ignored by those who disagreed at a more visceral level. Combining past precedent and recent testimony, he established that the guiding principle of British strategy after 1805 had been to counter Napoleon's naval forces: the need to retain command of sea made this the true concentration on the decisive theater. Unlike Mahan he did not think Trafalgar had ended the war at sea, Napoleon had not given up the contest until 1813, and Britain responded with a series of maritime offensives aimed at naval bases, fleets, and resources. These operations kept Britain secure, while hostile bases outside Europe were seized to reduce the loss of shipping and consequent economic damage and to open new outlets for trade and commerce. Britain defeated Napoleon's offensives and struck back, destroying his navy and opening new markets. The ultimate expression of this strategy came in Iberia, where the recovery of Portugal and support for the Spanish Revolt denied Napoleon the great naval bases at Lisbon and Cadiz. This strategy was the best use of Britain's limited military capability.

However Corbett made much larger points about the utility of history as a guide for current thinking and about the use of recent experience to help those grappling for the realities of past events. The First World War had changed his assessment of the Napoleonic conflict, leading him to argue that the true significance of Trafalgar had been obscured behind a wave of unthinking patriotism.

The implication is clear that, had he lived to complete volume four of the *Official History*, Corbett might have further developed his thesis on the "unimportance of battle," which was bitterly attacked as heresy after the inconclusive outcome of Jutland. Comparing German attacks on seaborne commerce with Napoleon's desperate search for a strategy after 1805 would have been consistent with his wider thinking and would have helped to shape what became, in lesser hands, a rambling narrative of losses and counterattacks. Corbett, and Corbett alone, could have rendered the latter stages of the naval war coherent and compelling at the strategic level. Obviously such a feat would not only have been consistent with the approach taken in *Some Principles*, it would also have advanced the writing of a new edition.

In his last engagement with the past Corbett tried to shock his audience, which included both naval officers and academics, out of the lazy assumptions that had led to the catastrophic losses between 1914 and 1918. Napoleon, the ultimate continental soldier, had failed to defeat Britain while the British operated alone, despite having conquered Western Europe. Britain survived and prospered because it adopted the correct time-honored strategy of limited maritime war. By avoiding continental commitments Britain avoided exposing itself to "decisive" military defeat. Sea power, he stressed, had not been secured at Trafalgar but merely confirmed. And such results were always temporary. Napoleon had tried again after 1805, and it required Britain's constant attention to maintain command of the sea—attention that involved both sea and land forces. In war the results are never secure until the fighting finally stops and the political process has been completed. Corbett demonstrated that, even after the "victory" that "assured" access, Britain still needed a national maritime strategy to guide the operations that sustained sea control until Napoleon was finally defeated.

The last two decades have witnessed wars in Iraq and Afghanistan, wars whose ruinous cost in lives and treasure was wholly disproportionate to their outcome. These wars cannot be ended by the "victors"; their legacy will endure for decades. Had a Corbettian account of the strategic history of the two regions as well as the bitter experience of those who had campaigned there previously been produced, it would have given those tasked with planning these conflicts pause for thought. To make our leaders wise and humble is perhaps the ultimate test for sound military education.

NAPOLEON AND THE BRITISH NAVY AFTER TRAFALGAR

April 1922

Seeing that it is hoped to revive the project of founding in the University of London a School of Naval History—a project which the late war held up—it seems appropriate on this occasion to select for the Creighton Lecture a subject which would indicate how much remains for such a school to do. Judged by the standards of modern historical scholarship, naval history between Trafalgar and Waterloo is a trackless desert. There are many other periods that have been no better worked, but the one we are about to consider probably surpasses all others in importance and instruction. So much may be said with confidence, not only because it is nearest to our own times, but also because of its striking analogy to the history we have recently been living. For a great part of the period it turned on a mortal commercial struggle, the issue of which for many exhausting years hung in the balance. This is but one of the analogies of which I have spoken, but I place it foremost for the sake of emphasising a special aim in the scheme it is hoped to inaugurate.

In defining the scope of the proposed School of Naval History it was never the idea that it should be concerned only with the operations of the Royal Navy. The word 'Naval' was intended to connote the whole activities of our life at sea. We already knew enough to appreciate that the successes of the Royal Navy owed much to the correlative enterprise of our oversea merchants and our mercantile marine. I need hardly tell how the experiences of our last war have deepened, illuminated, and intensified that impression. Here then is a further reason for the choice of my subject. Never perhaps were the resourcefulness, enterprise, and courage of our mercantile community a weightier factor in a great war than when they found themselves face to face with Napoleon's colossal

Julian S. Corbett, "Napoleon and the British Navy After Trafalgar," Creighton Memorial Lecture, *The Quarterly Review*, April 1922. Lecture delivered October 11, 1921.

system for boycotting our trade. Yet it is still the obscurest and least studied part of the story. It is the more to be regretted, for a main reason why Naval History has become so much a closed borough, in which the general historian seldom ventures to tread, is undoubtedly that our trade history has been so much divorced from Naval History. Yet in truth each must remain obscure out of the light of the other. They are, in fact, twins which can never be quite happy apart.

This is but one of the still dark aspects of my subject, and there are so many others that it is difficult to deal, even in outline, with all the accepted views which cry most loudly for revision. From Trafalgar to Waterloo is nearly ten years—obviously too big a canvas for one short lecture. I would, therefore, ask your main attention to the period following Nelson's victory, the period in which, after the Third Coalition collapsed, we were left to carry on the world-war practically alone.

Looked at from the purely military point of view (the only one, except perhaps the diplomatic, from which it has been studied) the course of the war seems to have violated all sound doctrine. Thus seen, it is a series of sporadic and apparently unrelated efforts in which our small army was used in driblets nearly all over the world with no consistent policy. No concentration of effort is visible anywhere; so that, in contrast with the justly admired conduct of the great military and political leader who was opposed to us, it all looks like amateurish child's play, and, as such, it is often dismissed with contempt. Yet it was this child's play that won, and won, as it seems, miraculously. For half the period which extended from the downfall of the Third Coalition to Elba, we had, practically single-handed, to face one of the greatest masters of war the world has ever seen, with nearly the whole of Europe at his back in subjection or alliance. Yet we survived in such vigour that we were in due time able to revive and in a great measure to finance the last Coalition, which finally brought our great adversary to his knees. How was it done, if all sound war doctrine was violated? Where the facts have been so imperfectly studied it would be idle to attempt a final judgment. But clearly revision is needed; and all I would endeavour to indicate is the line on which revision could proceed. It is not without hesitation that I do so. It is difficult to offer an apologia for the Government of the time without seeming to trench on the sanctity of a cardinal military principle; I mean the principle of concentrating the utmost possible force against the main strength of the enemy. So valuable and even sacred is this article of faith that even to seem to question its applicability to all possible conditions of war is to raise at once a cry of heresy. But here lies encouragement to proceed. A charge of heresy connotes the existence of dogma; and, of all diseases from which strategical thought can suffer, dogma is the most fatal. When dogma steals in at the door, reason flies out of the window. Principle always has a tendency to ossify into dogma; and, at the first symptom of such degradation being on foot, the application of a little historical massage may safely be prescribed.

On this occasion I would begin the treatment by quoting two dicta, one mediaeval with an almost devotional note, the other modern, practical and coldly scientific. The first is from 'The Libel of English Policy' written in 1436—

> 'Kepe well the sea that is the wall of England,
> And then is England kept by Goddes hand.'

The second is from Colonel Henderson, than whom, as a writer on war, I believe no higher authority exists in this country. In his 'Science of War' he lays down what he calls 'the great maxim that the naval strength of the enemy should be the first objective of the forces of a maritime Power, both by land and sea.' If now, without accepting this maxim as gospel, we apply it as a working hypothesis to the apparently confused conduct of the War, we find British policy assuming a very different aspect. We have at once a thread which binds the sporadic incidents into a consistent whole; and, in place of haphazard adventures, we get the impression of a concentration of effort in what proved to be at least one of the decisive theatres of the war.

To this view I can well imagine quick objection taken. Why, it may be asked, devote our slender army to assisting the navy to secure the command of the sea when we had already won it at Trafalgar? The objection is natural enough. So brilliant was the triumph in which the greatest Admiral of all time came to his end, that the dramatic sense of the historian almost compels him to ring down the curtain there and then. Even Mahan, for all his philosophic outlook, could not resist the temptation. It is on his works that intelligent appreciation of our sea-story mainly rests; and he stopped short at Trafalgar, as though it had finally shattered Napoleon's sea-power.

But did it? This was certainly not Napoleon's view. The Franco-Spanish fleet of Villeneuve, though stricken to impotency, was not destroyed. It was materially capable of regeneration. Napoleon had other fleets and squadrons undefeated. Other of his Allies, besides Spain, had ships, and certain weak neutrals had more. He was soon at work on schemes to restore his naval power out of these scattered elements; and we still have his minute calculations, culminating in that of 1808, which showed over 130 sail of the line within his reach for the next year. That the pictures he formed year by year were sanguine is not to be denied. But we ourselves, to judge at least by our building programmes, were scarcely less sensitive to the possibilities which Trafalgar had left open. In 1806 we had building or ordered 26 ships of the line. In 1807 the figure rose to 36. In the two following years it was as high as 48 and 47. Then it slowly fell, but it was not till 1812 that it was down again to 30. The cruiser programme was no less significant.

For Napoleon his dream was undoubtedly a real possibility. Nothing indeed gives a stronger impression of the abounding resource and energy of the man than to follow in his correspondence the little-known story of his untiring efforts to restore his navy. As from year to year the struggle grew more bitter, every port over which he had any influence, from Venice round to the Texel, was set to work on new construction and incessantly spurred to increased activity. Millions were lavished on building new dockyards, extending old ones, and increasing their defences. All Europe was ransacked for materials, labour, and crews. Performance always lagged behind his hopes; and yet enough was done to force us to counter with the fullest strain that our own yards and man-power would bear. I need hardly remind you that it was our desperate straits to find crews that was the immediate cause of bringing America into the war against us. Once, it is true, Napoleon had his doubts. In the exhausting winter of 1806 he ordered Decrés, his Minister of Marine, to form a number of battalions from his seamen and dockyardhands, telling him, 'I mean to reconquer my colonies on land.' But his determination to revive his navy soon returned, and the might of his personality was such that anything he thought possible we could not ignore. And so it was that, for years after Trafalgar, our navy and our army were absorbed in action to prevent Napoleon's dream being realised.

Together they did prevent it, but the curious thing is that there is scarcely one of the operations of that long struggle which either Service cares to dwell upon. Copenhagen, Walcheren, the Basque Roads, the Portugal expedition which ended in the Convention of Cintra—we regard them all as failures or something to be ashamed of. Similarly, too, the other class of combined expeditions—those against the colonies of France and her subject Allies. Judged by strict military dogma, they involved an heretical dispersal of strength away from the main forces of the enemy. But, judged as a means of securing our sea-power, they fall into place with the European enterprises as part of the great concentration of effort. When, within a year of Trafalgar, Napoleon's raiding squadrons were driven from the sea, there still remained the privateers acting from oversea bases; and, for all our cruisers could do, they remained a thorn in the side of our trade till the bases from which they worked were in our hands. Over and above this necessity for the vitality of our sea-power was the need for new markets and new sources of supply, in place of those of which Napoleon was depriving us.

To express the whole situation diagrammatically, we may say that Napoleon's policy, after he found it impossible to strike us a decisive blow by invasion, was to exhaust us by shutting out our trade from Europe; and by forcing on us simultaneously heavy naval expenditure by the menace of reviving his fleets. Our reply was to capture new markets, and to destroy the elements of his new navy in its ports by combined operations. It is at least possible to argue that our policy of using the army in this way was correct. That your utmost military strength should be concentrated upon the decisive military theatre is a principle not to be gainsaid, provided always your utmost strength is great enough to give hope of a decision. But no theatre can be called a decisive theatre if a decision in it is beyond your strength. And what at this time was our utmost strength compared with the vast hosts which our enemy could marshal against it? For us there was no decisive theatre anywhere within reach of the enemy's main forces, except the sea.

This was the first factor in the problem that Ministers had to solve. The second was that, so long as we maintained our dominant position at sea, Napoleon could not strike a decisive blow against us. The outlook, then, which they had to face was a war of exhaustion, at all events until future developments gave our diplomacy the means of reviving the Coalition. But when, after Austerlitz, Pitt rolled up the map of Europe, that was a remote, almost hopeless prospect. In any case the war must be long, and the side that could endure the longest would be the side to win. How, then, could our small army have been more profitably used than working hand-in-hand with the navy to prevent Napoleon from ever being able to strike the decisive blow, and by protecting and fostering our trade to give us the means of endurance?

Now, so far as time permits, I would ask your attention to points where the current view of the joint enterprises seems to need revision, and particularly to those which were aimed at keeping the country out of danger of a decisive blow. To visualise the problem more clearly, one cardinal fact in Napoleon's naval policy must be kept always in view. His chief hopes of restoring his navy lay in the North Sea. Brest, which had been the main dockyard of his predecessors, was so far removed from the sources of ship-building material, and its communications were so bad, that he quickly realised it could not be relied on. His sagacious grip of realities turned his mind to the north. The resources of Scandinavia and Northern Germany were essential to his purpose. Within reach of them must be his dockyard; and so he quickly set about creating in the Scheld a substitute for Brest. On Antwerp and Flushing he began at once to spend the bulk of his energy as a cradle for his new fleet; and Denmark and Sweden were marked down to provide the ships which he could not hope to build himself. This dominant fact the British Government, always acutely sensitive to naval developments north of the Dover defile, was of course quick to grasp; and in it lies the justification, or at least the explanation, of the policy which it promptly inaugurated.

The first round of the new contest was the Copenhagen expedition of 1807, but this was not actually the first instance of using the army for a definite naval object. That had been done in 1805, when Sir James

Craig's little expedition was sent to the Mediterranean. Its object was to prevent Napoleon's occupation of Italy spreading to Sicily; for, with Sicily in the enemy's hands, we could not at that time maintain our hold on the Mediterranean, and, if that hold was lost, not only would our vital Levant trade go with it, but Napoleon would be free to develop his fondest ambitions in the East. Slender as was the force employed, it succeeded. To quote Colonel Henderson again: 'An army supported by an invincible navy possesses a strength which is out of all proportion to its size . . . if intelligently directed.' It was a truth Napoleon was slow to recognise. He could not understand why the tide of his conquests was held up at the Straits of Messina. Again and again he angrily urged his brother to make an end of the puny obstruction. But Joseph could not even take Reggio on the Italian side. The Emperor lost his temper. 'That damned rock,' he wrote, 'is thwarting all my plans.' But it was not the rock. It was something else, which his genius could not or would not grasp. When the rock fell the barrier still stood firm.

It was in the initial phase, with this success to their credit, that Ministers resolved to use our 'disposal force,' as it was called—that is, the force they were organising out of the surplus not thought necessary for home defence—to save the Coalition from utter collapse after Jena. The idea was that it should operate from the Baltic against Napoleon's line of communications to stop his alarming advance against Russia, and encourage the Swedes and Prussians to hold out. The island of Rügen, in Swedish Pomerania, was to be its base; and there, early in July 1807, Lord Cathcart arrived with some 30,000 men. But it was too late. Before the rest of the expedition was ready to sail, the Tsar had signed the Treaty of Tilsit; and, save for Sweden, we were alone.

The naval danger was now acute. Under the Treaty of Tilsit the Continental System was inaugurated. By its secret articles Denmark, Sweden, Portugal, and Austria were to be compelled to adhere to it and enforce it with their fleets. Besides 17 sail of line, on which Napoleon could count in Dutch ports, the Swedes had 11, the Danes 16, and the Russians 60. On the Holstein frontier was Bernadotte with an army of 70,000 men, ready to coerce Denmark if she held back. I need hardly dwell on the gravity of the crisis. It meant not only the prospect of a formidable naval force based north of the Dover defile, which would render possible a descent upon Scotland or upon Ireland north-about, but it also meant our complete exclusion from the Baltic, the main source from which came our naval stores.

If there had been regrettable delay in preparing the Riigen expedition, there was none now. Never perhaps did our Government act with greater decision, speed, or secrecy. The Treaty of Tilsit was signed on July 9, 1807. On July 22 Canning heard directly from Tilsit of the intended maritime league against Great Britain, and was informed that Napoleon regarded the accession of Denmark as essential. With Bernadotte's army on the Danish frontier, there could be no doubt what this meant; and our Government saw that to forestall Napoleon was the only way to baffle his deadly plot. Invidious as was the high-handed action, a neutral unable to assert its neutrality must not become a tool in the enemy's hand. On what day the desperate decision was taken is not certain. On July 18 and 19 the Government had warned the Senior Naval Officer in the Baltic and also General Cathcart of their intention to ask Denmark to declare herself, and to back the demand by force. But when, on July 21, the orders of the Naval Commander-in-Chief, Admiral Gambier, were signed, they contained nothing about Copenhagen. His instructions were merely to defend Sweden, to protect trade, and reinforce Cathcart; but, as he was Senior Naval Lord of the Admiralty, he was probably in on the secret. Next day the news from Tilsit must have removed all doubt; on the 27th sailing orders were issued for the troops to proceed to Copenhagen.

To appreciate fully the dexterous handling of our disposal force in combination with the North-Sea Fleet, we should have to follow in detail its rapid and well organised movements. Here it must suffice to say that Napoleon was outwitted and out-manoeuvred. So little did he fathom the secret that, though Bernadotte was pressing for marching-orders, it was not till the last day of July that the Emperor called upon Denmark to make her choice. Next day the first echelon of our troops arrived. It was not till a week later that he heard of the expedition, and even then he did not divine its object. The orders he gave were for a concentration at Riigen and Emden; and though, owing to bad weather delaying the landing, Copenhagen did not capitulate till Sept. 6, he was powerless to save it and its precious fleet.

Every admirer of Napoleon must sympathise with his mortification. On July 4, three days before the Treaty of Tilsit was a certainty, he wrote to Decrés, urging him to speed up the new construction he had ordered, and he added, 'Everything points to the Continental war being at an end. Our whole effort must now be thrown on the naval side.' That was the form the great struggle was now to take; and we had got in the first blow. In the full radiance of his new triumph he had been caught napping; his new system, on which he relied to bring the enemy to submission, had received a deep wound before it was born. He could do nothing to heal it; and all his vexation was concentrated in a propaganda—such as we now understand so well—to brand us as ruthless oppressors of neutrals and international outlaws. He had made all preparations to do what we had done, but we had been too quick for him; and that was the unpardonable sin. So the propaganda spread; and not only did it fix Continental opinion for a century, but, curiously enough, it sank so deep into the ears of our historians that to this day they can only approach the exploit with shame-faced apologies. It is always treated with blushes as an easy victory over little, unsuspecting Denmark. The world has forgotten that it was a very difficult victory over the great, unsuspecting Napoleon.

Our activity did not end with the capture of the Danish fleet and keeping the Baltic open. Mercantile enterprise had also played its part. No sooner was the boycott project known than our merchants set about making a hole in it for themselves. Smuggling was then a fine art. There was little they did not know about it. All they required was a base of operations in some no-man's land. Denmark had declared war, and the Danish island of Heligoland was ideal for the purpose; and at their suggestion it was seized by a naval force the day before Copenhagen capitulated. Thus they established a smuggling station. The tale of what went on there I cannot tell. It is one of the points that still await research, but Napoleon's constant complaint of the increasing leak that continued to exist in its vicinity suggests that research would be amply repaid. We know at least that three years later the leak had grown so serious that Napoleon had to order the entrances of the Jahde, Weser, and Elbe to be fortified, and each provided with a flotilla to stop the Heligoland smuggling. He was also asking Decrés if a ship of the line could not be stationed at Cuxhaven, and was calling for a plan for taking the obnoxious island with a cruiser squadron entering the North Sea northabout and combining with the Cuxhaven flotilla.

The rest of the story in the North is how De Saumarez held the Baltic till the danger passed. That was when Russia broke away from the Continental System at the urgent entreaty of her impoverished merchants. It is a page of our naval history too little known and still inadequately studied. Besides De Saumarez's own remarkable exploits and even more remarkable diplomacy, there is the mercantile enterprise that he made possible. In the Baltic, too, smuggling stations were established, and their story still remains to be unraveled. We only know what came of it from a graphic glimpse at the time, when in 1810 Bernadotte passed into Sweden as Crown Prince elect. On reaching the Belt he found De Saumarez there in the 'Victory,' and had to ask his leave to cross over to his prospective kingdom. It was given, and he passed on with unconcealed admiration through a British homeward-bound convoy of over 1000 merchantmen. I am not suggesting for a moment that we did not feel the Continental System severely for a time. No one, I believe, at this moment could speak with confidence as to how far it affected our trade and finance. All I would say is that knowledge of it has been mainly the province of international lawyers. Of its commercial effects, the methods by which our merchants fought it under cover of the navy, the extent of their success, we have as yet but glimpses. The whole story is yet to be told.

To return to the general policy of the Government, the intention was to follow up Copenhagen with an attack on the Scheld with the disposal force under Lord Wellesley, in order to secure the Franco-Dutch fleet and dockyards to which Napoleon was devoting ever increasing exertions at Antwerp and Flushing; and this again was to be succeeded by an attack on Cadiz to deal with what Trafalgar had left of Villeneuve's fleet. But it was not to be. In any case, it was too near the well known season of Walcheren fever for Flushing to be attempted so late in the year; but the real cause of the interruption of our programme was the direct outcome of Napoleon's active reply to Copenhagen.

Foiled in the Baltic, he turned with one of his characteristic and formidable changes of front to the Mediterranean; and there sprang up in his unteachable brain another of those naval combinations which, however impracticable we may have learned to regard them, compel our admiration of his indomitable spirit. Whatever we may now think of them, they were then formidable enough to call for our utmost energy to defeat them. His first step was to order Marshal Junot, who had been concentrating an army for the purpose at Bayonne, to march on Lisbon in order to seize the Portuguese fleet and the Tagus. As a naval base, the Tagus was far too valuable to be allowed to fall into the enemy's hands. An attempt to save it with a combined force was imperative; and for this reason all idea of attempting the fleets in the Scheld and Cadiz had to be given up for the present.

Portugal was then neutral; and we had before us the unpleasant prospect of another edition of Copenhagen. But diplomacy found a way out. We offered, if Napoleon's demands were refused, to escort the Court and fleet to Brazil, and to send a military force to cover the departure. This offer, after much difficulty, was accepted; and finally, on Nov. 29, when Junot was already in sight of the city, the withdrawal was effected, and twelve ships of war, on which Napoleon had counted, were lost to him. But the Tagus had to be given up to Junot, and in it a Russian squadron of nine ships of the line. This squadron, until the Treaty of Tilsit was signed, had been operating under Seniavin with our own squadron at the Dardanelles, and had slipped into Lisbon on its way to the Baltic for fear of the British fleet. There we had to blockade it till the coming of the expedition with which we hoped to restore the situation. The task proved easier than we anticipated. Both Spain and Portugal were soon in a state of revolt. The end of the episode was the beginning of the Peninsular War, when on Aug. 30, 1808, the Convention of Cintra gave us our old base in the Tagus, and removed Seniavin's squadron into a British port for the duration of war.

But, after all, this was but a part of Napoleon's plan for doing in the Mediterranean what he had failed to do in the Baltic. His idea was in effect an elaborate combination of military and naval force for surprising Sicily and thereby depriving us of the power to maintain a fleet within the Straits. Three or four armies were to be thrown against the island simultaneously from Calabria, Naples, Toulon, and possibly

Corfu, which was now his, and which we were blockading. They were to move under cover of a naval concentration which was first intended to be in the Tagus, but, when under pressure of our fleet and diplomacy Portugal proved obstructive, was to be made in the Mediterranean. There were to meet Allemand from Rochefort, Rosily from Cadiz, Ganteaume from Toulon, and a Spanish squadron from Cartagena; the whole to be covered by a revival of the invasion threat from Boulogne and Napoleon's other flotilla ports. To the success of this design the whole force of his genius was directed. 'Sicily,' he told his brother Joseph, in trying to inflame him with his own fire, 'Sicily is the most important point in the world.' For him Sicily, in fact, was the decisive theatre; but the plan failed, for the naval concentration broke down. Only Allemand and Ganteaume succeeded in meeting; and all they did was to relieve Corfu. Collingwood was rigidly guarding Sicily, and only by a hair's breadth did they escape him. But they did get away back to Toulon; and the failure to intercept them 'broke poor Collingwood's heart.' But his vigilance had saved 'the most important point in the world'; and the revolt of Spain then put it beyond Napoleon's power to revive his plan. A further consequence for ourselves was that a combined expedition against Cadiz was no longer required. On June 14, ten days after the Provisional Government at Seville had declared war on France, Rosily, who was blockaded by a British squadron of ten ships of the line, surrendered to the Spaniards.

Rapidly as the elements on which Napoleon based his hope of regaining his sea-power were falling away, his high resolution was undefeated. Plan after plan came from his fertile brain. According to one scheme, which involved an entirely new combination, Ganteaume, starting from Toulon, was to open all the blockaded Atlantic ports in succession, and then to proceed to the Channel—if possible to the Scheld—and there cover a new attempt to invade by means of the restored Boulogne flotilla and two expeditionary forces from the Texel and Flushing. It is hardly possible that Napoleon really believed such a plan to be practicable. His idea most probably was only to intimidate and exhaust us till his new fleet was ready.

In this year (1808) he was calculating, with new constructions, to see 130 of the line at his disposal in 1809. It was the year 1809, moreover, that saw the last of his sanguine naval combinations, a slightly varied repetition of what he had attempted in the year of Trafalgar. All his remaining squadrons were to meet in the West Indies or Brazil; but the plan had even less success than its prototype. The Brest squadron alone was able to break out, and it was so hotly pressed that it had to take refuge in the Basque Roads. What happened to it there—the story of Cochrane's explosion vessels—is well known. It remains in our history as a failure, because Gambier, who had managed well enough at Copenhagen, shrank at the last moment from going in to complete what the explosion vessels had only half done. But in French history it survives as a crushing defeat. Allemand, the only Admiral besides Ganteaume in whom Napoleon now had any faith, had been summoned from Toulon to organise the defence. So drastic were his methods that he completely gutted both ships and dockyard to construct his booms and other defences; and the result was that the squadron could never be made fit for service again.

There now remained to Napoleon little more than his Toulon and Antwerp squadrons. From that of Toulon we had nothing to fear. With our hold on Sicily secure, and Minorca and other Spanish ports at our disposal, we held it in a vice. But Antwerp was another matter. The squadron there now consisted of twenty good sail of the line, with several more in course of construction; and, so long as it existed, we were forced to provide against the possibility of a descent on our northern coasts. If we were to be free for offensive operations in support of our new Allies and to concentrate with them against the armed forces of the enemy, the eradication of the menace was a necessary preliminary, and it could not be done without the army. But was it now justifiable to use our disposal force to stamp out the last spark of Napoleon's naval hopes? Conditions had changed. We were no longer single-handed. In Spain we had an ally and a theatre for promising military operations. Austria too had once more taken the field. Should we not rather have reverted to orthodox methods against the enemy's army? That question is the question of Walcheren.

The Walcheren episode is a *locus classicus*. It was the largest combined expedition we had ever organised, and it is the one most consistently ridiculed. Yet Colonel Henderson could say that, though it failed, it was, on his principle of the naval strength of the enemy being the first objective of both our land and our sea forces, 'a strategical stroke of the highest order.' But was it entirely a failure, and was it undertaken on the principle he lays down? In naval opinion the squadron was certainly the objective. But military and political opinion seem to have been swayed by more far-reaching aims. Napoleon was denuding France and all his western front of troops to deal rapidly with Austria; a stream of intelligence told of growing antipathy to his domination in all quarters; and there is little doubt that the surprise of the port on which his main hopes rested would have produced a moral shock to his prestige that was worth a big effort and no little risk.

Although the majority of our narratives, whose main authority appears to have been the opposition Press of the time, assert the contrary, it was a surprise. French contemporary evidence, and particularly the correspondence between Decrés and General Clarke at the War Office, leave no doubt about the matter. They, of course, knew that an expedition was preparing and were watching it anxiously, but what its objective was they could not make out. In turn their conjectures varied as widely as from the Mediterranean to the Baltic. Rochefort, Brest, the Scheld, Kronstadt—each in turn seemed indicated as the most likely guess, but the Scheld was never high in the betting, and nothing was done to guard it. Decrés' last word to Napoleon, just before the expedition sailed, was that he could not tell its objective, but had little doubt it was in the north. Even when he got by telegraph news that our troops were landing in force, he was not believed and Clarke did nothing. A week elapsed before the startling information reached Napoleon at Schonbrunn; and it was not till Aug. 7, two days after Wagram, that, at three o'clock in the morning, he drafted orders for Bernadotte to hurry to the scene of danger and take command by land and sea. Ten days more went by before Bernadotte reached Antwerp; and then it was to find everything in chaos and Flushing in our hands.

For nearly three weeks Antwerp lay at our mercy; and the primary cause of the failure was not military but naval. A sudden break in the weather prevented the landing of troops to seize Cadsand on the south bank of the river; and that was the first stage of the plan of operations. The result was that the ships could not go in as intended till Flushing had been reduced, and the transports had to seek refuge from the gale in the East Scheld instead of proceeding direct to the head of the main estuary. But for that unlucky flaw of bad weather, Antwerp would have been an easy prey, as Napoleon well knew and afterwards confessed. During the past twelve months the defences of his new port had been a continual source of anxiety. About Cadsand he was particularly anxious. 'In all my Empire,' he wrote to Decrés, 'this is the weakest point, and the only one at which it is possible to deal me a blow.' Decrés was to do his best to provide a force for its protection, but no troops could be kept there permanently because of the fever. The gale gave time for its defences to be occupied, and Flushing had to be reduced before the troops could enter the river. The delay proved fatal and very costly in precious lives.

Still, had the chief commanders shown the energy and accepted the risks that Keats and Hope did in their brilliant seizure of South Beveland, all might have been well. So near, indeed, did it come to complete success, so well laid was the elaborate plan, that even the failure gave Napoleon an acute attack of nerves. A few days after he heard of the fall of Flushing he sent a peremptory order to his Director of Conscription, telling him he must organise a force of 500,000 of the National Guard permanently in seven armies. Otherwise all the French armies will be consumed in defending the coasts. 'With 300 sail of transports,' he wrote, 'and 50,000 men in the Downs, England can paralyse 300,000 of our troops, and will reduce us to the rank of a second-class Power.' We need not take him too seriously, but his outburst reads significantly beside his previous gibes at our sporadic expeditions as 'the combinations of pygmies.'

There is no doubt that, even after the first shock had passed, he felt the blow keenly. The Scheld was the centre of his naval hopes; but without Flushing, where, before leaving, we had completely destroyed the port and arsenal, Antwerp, for technical reasons, was of little value either as a base or a dockyard. It was for this reason Napoleon seized the place after Trafalgar, and continued to lavish care and treasure upon it. In the budget of this year he had allotted a million to the Scheld, half of which was for Flushing. As soon as he knew we were evacuating Walcheren, he issued a decree for forming a new large basin at Antwerp and for reconstructing the demolished port of Flushing. For a time he still kept up his heart. The naval budget for 1810 was 110 millions; and Decrés was expected to have over 100 ships of the line by 1812. After this his note lowered. In 1811 he still kept urging Decrés to press on his programme, and issued orders for conscripting dock labourers. But his resources were not equal to the strain. All he could hope now was for 100 ships of the line and 200 frigates in four years' time, with which he would wrest from England her supremacy at sea. That we may take as his naval swan-song. Before those four years were out he was in Elba. Indeed, the policy we had been pursuing had been so effective that, after Walcheren, our fleet was able to devote its main energy for the rest of the war to supporting the army in the Peninsula. To that the Admiralty gave its chief attention, and so made full return for what the army had done for the navy. The fleet henceforth was made subordinate to the army, its nurse and hand-maid, as Wellington handsomely confessed when he learned how much it had done for him.

The extent of the Admiralty effort has never been worked out; and here undoubtedly is further need for revision. The current belief that Wellington's communications were not safe rests mainly on complaints he made when, after Vittoria, he suddenly changed his base from Lisbon to the awkward little port of Passages on the north coast. But the complaint was unjustified; it rested on inaccurate information. When the Admiralty inquired into the matter it was found that during the months of August, September, and October of 1813—the period of the loudest complaint and the greatest throng of transport traffic—only two ships had been captured, one of which had apparently strayed from her convoy, while the other had been snapped up by an American privateer. That there had been a short period of insecurity is true, but it was because secrecy was so vital to Wellington's brilliant movement which culminated at Vittoria, that he had refrained from telling the Admiralty or the Commander-in-Chief of the change of the base thrown out of gear and could not be rearranged in a moment. When all this was fully explained to Wellington, his tone completely changed. 'If any one,' he said in thanking Admiral Martin, 'wishes to know the history of this war, I will tell him our maritime superiority gives me the power of maintaining my communications while the enemy is unable to do so'—a remark which gives a very different colour to the current impression.

Many other points in the naval story of the Peninsular War call equally for deeper study, but here I must conclude the crude sketch which is all I have been able to attempt. It has been well said that current history the history we have lived ourselves—is as illuminating for past history as is past history for enriching the experience of our own days. It is certainly true of the vivid, almost dazzling light with which the last years of the late war flood the period of my lecture. Seen in the new light, it looks as though nearly every current belief about the later exhausting years of our struggle with Napoleon needs modification—even the cardinal belief, the effect of Trafalgar. Going even lightly over the ground, its striking analogy to our latest struggle brings forth a whole harvest of unsettled queries; and the one which for me at least is the most insistent is this: What material advantage did Trafalgar give that Jutland did not give? It is one that, in the present state of our knowledge, I will not venture to answer.

CONCLUSION

At the heart of Corbett's thinking on war, strategy, and policy were a set of imperatives. The development of sound national strategy required the sustained interaction of academic history and theoretical strategic principles, with historians and strategists working in an environment of mutual esteem as equal, professional partners in an enterprise that blended the detachment of the university with the present-minded rigor of Service Academy. Today that model is widely accepted, and Corbett's many intellectual descendants provide navies with vital tools that inform their thinking. It was no accident that his unpublished masterpiece on the Russo-Japanese War was rescued from obscurity by the two eminent Corbettian Service educators and the Naval Institute Press.[1]

Corbett's work achieved considerable international recognition in his lifetime. Before 1914 *Some Principles* was a core text at the U.S. Naval War College. Between the wars French theorist Admiral Raoul Castex attempted to develop Corbett's ideas. The other major interwar thinkers Admiral Sir Herbert Richmond and Herbert Rosinski promoted his concepts. Corbett's subtle, sophisticated elucidation of maritime strategy was revived in the blustering journalese of Basil Liddell Hart's "British Way in Warfare," based on extensive coaching by Corbett's old friend Herbert Richmond. British Grand Strategy in the Second World War was more Corbettian than it had been in the First World War, using command of the sea to keep the enemy divided—moving armies and air forces over vast distances and then landing from the sea to defeat them one by one. In the nuclear age his limited war theory reemerged as the only strategic choice in an age of mutually assured destruction. The decades since the end of the Cold War have brought limited war back into focus. Indeed the shift was presaged by the Falklands Conflict of 1982, a case study that demonstrated the genius of *Some Principles*. That the British state persisted with a distinctly continental defense policy for another three decades suggests Corbett's message had been lost in the communication overload about conflict and security. Perhaps the shorter format might have been better suited to convey his ideas.

I hope this volume has demonstrated Corbett's formidable skill as an essayist, his ability to challenge flawed ideas and weak arguments with clarity and logic as he targeted critical audiences beyond the worlds of naval history and strategic theory. Corbett's essays should be required reading for civilians commenting on defense: his unerring ability to address specific audiences, work with confidential evidence, and sustain his own opinions sustained "Jacky" Fisher's policy at a critical period and upheld the primacy of national strategy. Corbett conceived these essays within a larger context; they helped to shape his work on strategic doctrine.

Modern commentators and thinkers on defense issues can learn a great deal from the way Corbett developed his writing. He steadily developed his understanding of strategy through a series of historically based but forward-looking case studies—studies that traced the evolution of ideas and methods—while refining his analysis using the debating skills honed in his legal career. In the modern age of digital media and instant gratification it is tempting to overvalue other disciplines that appear to offer quick answers, but such disciplines have consistently proven to be an inadequate base for strategic doctrine, sound military thought, and action. Mahan, Corbett, and Clausewitz are as one in valuing the intelligent analysis of the past above all other methods of comprehending war and strategy. They remain core reading because the hard lessons of war have only confirmed their wisdom. Alternative offerings, driven by universalizing theoretical models, have little value for specific countries and specific problems. Does anyone not realize that a thorough investigation of British and Russian experience in Afghanistan would have saved many lives and billions of dollars/pounds? Corbett's message was clear: history had taught the British not to engage in large-scale continental warfare. He was ignored, and the consequences were catastrophic for Britain. A long-term relationship with such sophisticated thinkers is essential to sound military decision making. Men like Corbett do not decide, instead they ensure decisions are taken with eyes wide open, dangers explained, and precedents demonstrated.

Consequently these essays would enhance any program within professional military education or the university studying strategy, policy, and the interrelationship between past and present. Corbett's writings demonstrate the importance of connecting the intellectual life of armed forces, the academy, and the nation in the search for coherent policy, strategy, and doctrine. His insistence on building national strategy on the hard lessons of past experience, and elevating that experience above the parochial contemporary concerns of individual armed forces and Service rivalries, depended on accurate scholarship and sound theoretical analysis. He used the past to test contemporary arguments. His career demonstrated that the interplay of ideas and experience, when intellectuals and warriors worked together, was of estimable mutual benefit. He did much to establish the role of civilians in modern Service education, not least because he openly admitted the limits of his knowledge and never aspired to teach his students their job.

Above all Corbett was anxious that junior and midcareer naval and military officers should be encouraged and equipped to think. He knew that without such encouragement it was unrealistic to expect them to show much imagination at flag rank. His greatest criticism of the admirals of his day was not that they were stupid—very few of them were—but that their limited, largely technical, education had not equipped them to deal with the dogma and cant of the age or to reach logical deductions. The work of men like Corbett, Mahan, Clausewitz, Ellis, and many others, can help our sailors and soldiers become the intelligent warriors that our nations need in the twenty-first century. That task has not changed across time. The reading lists for advanced defense education in 1914 included many of the same texts lists contain today. That is no accident. Following fashion is fine for couture, not for war. Corbett teaches us how to integrate the best methods and ideas from the past with the latest thinking and experience, and that has always been the best place from which to plot a course for the future. His works are the ultimate expression of sea power thinking, created in the last great sea empire at the apogee of its power. They stand alongside Thucydides.

NOTES

Introduction: Making National Strategy

1. Donald M. Schurman, *Julian S. Corbett, 1854–1922: Historian of British Maritime Policy from Drake to Jellicoe* (London: Royal Historical Society, 1981); J. J. Widen, *Theorist of Maritime Strategy: Sir Julian Corbett and His Contribution to Military and Naval Thought* (Farnham: Ashgate, 2012) provides an important assessment of his theoretical work.

2. Julian S. Corbett, *Some Principles of Maritime Strategy* (London: Longmans, 1911). The latest edition, edited by Eric Grove, was publishcd by thc Naval Institute Press in 1988. All references in the paper to *Some Principles* are to the 1988 Annapolis edition.

3. Schurman, *Julian S. Corbett*, 17.

4. Corbett, *Some Principles*, 95, 97, 99, 102.

5. Andrew D. Lambert, "The Naval War Course, *Some Principles of Maritime Strategy* and the Origins of the 'British Way in Warfare,'" in *The British Way in Warfare: Power and the International System, 1856–1956: Essays in Honour of David French*, ed. Keith Neilson and Greg Kennedy (Farnham: Ashgate, 2010), 219–56.

6. Julian S. Corbett, "The Teaching of Naval and Military History," *History* April 1916.

7. Julian S. Corbett, War Course Lecture Spanish Succession October 1903, CBT Liddell-Hart Centre for Military Archives, Kings College London.

8. Julian S. Corbett, *England in the Seven Years' War: A Study in Combined Strategy*, vol. 1 (London: Longman, 1907), v–vii.

9. Julian S. Corbett, "War Course Lecture Dutch War I" (Liddell-Hart Centre for Military Archives, Kings College London, December 1913).

10. Peter Paret, "The Genesis of *On War*," in *On War*, ed. and trans. Michael Howard and Peter Paret (Princeton, NJ: Princeton University Press, 1976), 24.

11. Corbett recognized the key weakness of Clausewitz's work, which he attributed to its unfinished state and the inability to explain the distinctive character of limited war. Corbett, *Seven Years' War*, vol. 1:207n1. This is the first statement of what became the dominant theme of Part One of *Some Principles*.

12. He only mentioned Mahan twice in *Some Principles*, 1988, 131n and 169, using specific examples to illustrate strategic concentration and control of communications.

13. William S. Sims letter to Corbett, September 10, 1918, 30 Grosvenor Square, London, CBT Corbett Papers, National Maritime Museum London, January 2, 1936.

14. Corbett letter to Fisher, December 6, 1918, in *Fear God III* (London: Cape, 1956), 538–39. The correspondence was a response to Fisher's paper "The Strangest Thing in the War."

15. Sir Michael Howard's *The Continental Commitment: The Dilemma of the British Defence Policy in the Era of the Two World Wars* (London: Penguin, 1972) is the basis of these arguments.

Chapter 1. Defending the Admiralty and Disposing of Discontent

1. Fisher to Arnold White, December 31, 1906, in ed. A. J. Marder, *Fear God and Dreadnought : The Correspondence of Admiral of the Fleet Lord Fisher of Kilverstone*, Vol. 2, *Years of Power, 1904–1910* (London: Jonathan Cape 1956), 109.

Chapter 3. The Role of Maritime International Law in Grand Strategy

1. Julian S. Corbett, introduction to *Running the Blockade*, by Thomas E. Taylor (London: Murray, 1896), vii.

2. Julian Corbett, "The Capture of Private Property at Sea," *The Nineteenth Century and After*, June 1907. Reprinted in A. T. Mahan, *Some Neglected Aspects of War* (Boston: 1907); Donald M. Schurman, *Julian S. Corbett, 1854–1922: Historian of British Maritime Policy from Drake to Jellicoe* (London: Royal Historical Society, 1981), 71.

3. Earl Loreburn, *Capture at Sea* (London: Methuen, 1913).

Chapter 4. Doctrine—the Soul of Warfare

1. Julian S. Corbett, "Staff Histories," in *Naval and Military Essays: Being Papers Read at the Naval and Military Section of the International Congress of Historical*

Studies, ed. J. S. Corbett and H. J. Edwards (Cambridge: University of Cambridge Press, 1914), 24. Paper delivered in 1913.

2. Ibid., 26–27.

3. Ibid., 32–33.

Chapter 5. The Origins of Modern Naval History

1. Andrew D. Lambert, *"The Foundations of Naval History": Sir John Laughton, the Royal Navy and the Historical Profession* (London: Chatham Publishing, 1997).

2. Andrew D. Lambert, *The Crimean War: British Grand Strategy against Russia 1853–1856.* (Manchester: Manchester University Press, 1990; 2nd edition, Farnham: Ashgate, 2011).

Chapter 6. Defending Sea Power

1. Julian S. Corbett, "The Paradox of Imperialism," *Monthly Review* (October 1900): 1–14.

2. Julian S. Corbett, "The Sea Commonwealth," in *The Sea Commonwealth and other Papers*, ed. Arthur P. Newton (London: J. M. Dent & Sons, 1919), 8–10.

3. Julian S. Corbett, "The League of Nations and the Freedom of the Seas," pamphlet (Oxford: Oxford University Press, 1918).

Conclusion

1. Julian S. Corbett, *Maritime Operations in the Russo-Japanese War 1904–1905*, ed. J. Hattendorf and D. M. Schurman (Annapolis, MD: Naval Institute Press, 1994).

ABOUT THE EDITOR

Andrew Lambert is Laughton Professor of Naval History in the Department of War Studies at King's College, London, and Director of the Laughton Naval History Unit. He has taught at a number of British universities and defense academies. His work focuses on the naval and strategic history of the British Empire between the Napoleonic Wars and World War I. His most recent books include *The Crimean War: British Grand Strategy against Russia 1853–1856* and *The Challenge: Britain versus America in the Naval War of 1812*, winner of the Anderson Medal of the Society for Nautical Research.

The Naval Institute Press is the book-publishing arm of the U.S. Naval Institute, a private, nonprofit, membership society for sea service professionals and others who share an interest in naval and maritime affairs. Established in 1873 at the U.S. Naval Academy in Annapolis, Maryland, where its offices remain today, the Naval Institute has members worldwide.

Members of the Naval Institute support the education programs of the society and receive the influential monthly magazine *Proceedings* or the colorful bimonthly magazine *Naval History* and discounts on fine nautical prints and on ship and aircraft photos. They also have access to the transcripts of the Institute's Oral History Program and get discounted admission to any of the Institute-sponsored seminars offered around the country.

The Naval Institute's book-publishing program, begun in 1898 with basic guides to naval practices, has broadened its scope to include books of more general interest. Now the Naval Institute Press publishes about seventy titles each year, ranging from how-to books on boating and navigation to battle histories, biographies, ship and aircraft guides, and novels. Institute members receive significant discounts on the Press' more than eight hundred books in print.

Full-time students are eligible for special half-price membership rates. Life memberships are also available.

For a free catalog describing Naval Institute Press books currently available, and for further information about joining the U.S. Naval Institute, please write to:

Member Services
U.S. Naval Institute
291 Wood Road
Annapolis, MD 21402-5034
Telephone: (800) 233-8764
Fax: (410) 571-1703
Web address: www.usni.org